ATTENTION BOOK WRITER:

Mediterranean Diet Guide and Recipe Book for beginners

Easy and Healthy Everyday Mediterranean Diet Recipes

(includes 7-days meal plan)

by Victoria Prado

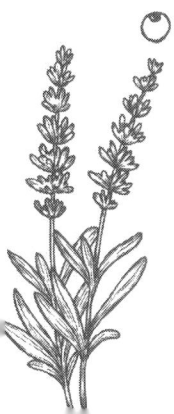
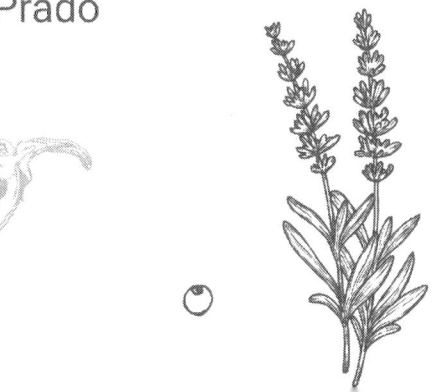

Copyright © 2020, by Victoria Prado
All rights reserved.

ISBN: 9798643545668

Acknowledgments

Iryna Kyrnoz for her help in creating the design of this book.

Table of Contents

INTRODUCTION 5

Chapter 1	*The Mediterranean Diet*	7
Chapter 2	*The Mediterranean Lifestyle*	11
Chapter 3	*Mediterranean Diet Pyramid*	17
Chapter 4	*The Benefits of the Mediterranean Diet*	25
Chapter 5	*Starting the Mediterranean Diet*	31
Chapter 6	*7-Day Meal Planning*	39
Chapter 7	*Breakfast Recipes*	43
Chapter 8	*Lunch and Dinner*	53
Chapter 9	*Side dishes and Soups*	87
Chapter 10	*Desserts*	101

CONCLUSION 111

Introduction

This delectable Mediterranean diet cookbook gives you 130 simple and filling meals packed with fresh fish, seafood, vegetables, fruits, whole grains, and heart-healthy fats traditional to Italy, Spain, and Greece. This Mediterranean diet book is the ultimate guide for delicious and quick Mediterranean recipes. The Mediterranean diet includes some of the most delicious recipes in the world. Once you try these recipes, you may want to stick to them because you're guaranteed to enjoy them. This cookbook will enable you to spend less time cooking and have more time for other things.

Recent scientific data shows that most people in the U.S and Europe are suffering from various form of artery blockage, atherosclerosis, and cardiac disease. This is where the Mediterranean diet is a lifesaver. The Mediterranean diet is one of the healthiest diets that both keeps your heart healthy and helps you lose weight at the same time. The Mediterranean diet focuses on consuming whole grains, fresh fruits, vegetables, fish, seafood, and a good amount of olive oil while eliminating any processed foods and sugar that would cause harm to your heart.

This diet program is unique in a way that it asks you to follow a healthy diet and incorporate a healthy lifestyle and social activates to ensure that you lead a prolonged and healthy life. This handy Mediterranean cookbook will show you how you can incorporate healthy recipes even on a busy weeknight. With simple recipes and flavorful ingredients, this diet cookbook will bring savory Mediterranean flavors to your plate and extra time to your day.

CHAPTER 1

The Mediterranean Diet

CHAPTER 1

The Mediterranean diet is known as the healthiest in the world. The Mediterranean diet is based on the specific cuisines of the regional countries surrounding the Mediterranean Sea, namely Greece, Italy, Cyprus, Spain, Morocco, Lebanon, France, and Portugal. However, it's more than a diet - it's a lifestyle that suggests a ton of things we should eat, and a little of things we shouldn't, along with shared physical and social activities. The Mediterranean diet is a culinary tradition that focuses on fresh fruits, vegetables, fish, seafood, whole grains, nuts, and olive oil with the occasional glass of red wine.

The Mediterranean diet is based on a simple premise: eat fresh, whole foods, in season. The Mediterranean diet idea is holistic and straightforward: eat more fish (especially fish that are rich with omega-3 fatty acids) and less meat.

Cook with olive oil, and eat whole grains, fresh fruits, and vegetables several times a day. The nuts included in the Mediterranean diet provide a good amount of monounsaturated and polyunsaturated fats. The Mediterranean diet omits processed foods, excessive amounts of saturated fat, trans fat, and refined sugar, while it includes moderate quantities of cheese, yogurt, red meat, and red wine.

The Mediterranean diet isn't specifically intended for rapid weight loss. Instead, it offers a way of eating that focuses on wholesome, nutritious foods that will satisfy your hunger and appetite while helping you achieve and sustain your optimal weight, as well as improve your overall health. In sum, it's a lifestyle that you can adopt today and maintain for the rest of your life.

The History of the Mediterranean Diet

The Mediterranean diet isn't tied to a particular country. Each region (Morocco, Southern France, Southern Italy, Spain, and Greece) has a different version of the diet, depending on the local produce and availability of ingredients. A biologist – Dr. Ancel Keys first studied the Mediterranean diet in the 1950s. In 1958, scientist Dr. Ancel Keys conducted a study - known as "the Seven Countries Study" - to find a correlation between cholesterol and heart disease.

The study included Japan, the United States, Finland, Italy, the Netherlands, Greece, and the former Yugoslavia. Keys posited that poor people in Southern Italy's small towns were generally healthier than rich people living in New York, including those who had emigrated from the previously mentioned Southern Italian towns. Keys' study showed that while the men from Finland showed a heart disease rate of 28% after 10 years, only 2% of the men from the Greek Island of Crete had developed heart disease. The difference between the diets of the two cultures was that the Cretans' saturated fat consumption was significantly lower. According to the research, the Greeks were getting close to half of their dietary fats from monounsaturated fats like olive oil, as well as large doses of omega-3 fatty acids from fish, nuts, and seeds. These healthy fats help to lower cholesterol levels and reduce the risk of heart disease. Over the course of the study, the Cretan men were shown to live the longest of any of the groups studied.

The Cretan diet was and is now very much in line with the diets of other cultures surrounding the Mediterranean – lots of olive oil, as well as whole grains, beans, and legumes, fresh vegetables and fruit, fish and other lean protein, and moderate quantities of cheese, eggs, milk, and red wine. The food is generally plant-based, fresh, and unprocessed. This is the essential makeup of the Mediterranean diet: complex carbohydrates, healthy fats, and plenty of vitamins, minerals, fiber, antioxidants, and phytochemicals.

Keys' finding was published in 1975. However, the Mediterranean diet became popular again in the 1990s when the Mayo Clinic, the Harvard School of Public Health, and the European office of the World Health Organization recognized the Mediterranean diet as the healthiest in the world. In 2013, UNESCO named this diet pattern an "Intangible Cultural Heritage" of Portugal, Spain, Italy, Greece, Morocco, Cyprus, and Croatia.

CHAPTER 2

The Mediterranean Lifestyle

CHAPTER 2

As mentioned earlier, the Mediterranean diet isn't merely a diet; in reality, it's a lifestyle - a healthy, active, and emotionally rich lifestyle. Diet is certainly a big part of what makes the Mediterranean region so healthy. However, the overall lifestyle of the Mediterranean is also important to the success of this eating plan. The people who live in the Mediterranean basin have a very different approach to life. Many often walk and bike to work, making their days more active; this lifestyle further increases their physical wellbeing.

People typically enjoy relaxed meals with their families, often accompanied by red wine. Each meal is seen as a feast and food is made and enjoyed together. Family and friends sit down to enjoy and celebrate meals such as breakfast, lunch, and dinner, and the food is never rushed. This time spent eating with family and friends gives you daily doses of healthy social interactions and contributes to feeling emotionally fulfilled. Mediterranean people target their errands on food, buying fresh, locally grown produce from neighborhood shops and markets and stopping to chat with neighbors and friends.

Instead of spending hours commuting in traffic, they devote their time out and about in town. Rather eating lunch hunched over their office computer, most people walk home to enjoy a meal with their families. The Mediterranean diet is a wholesome diet that's full of flavors and colors. It'll not only leave you satiated but also feeling healthy and more physically fit when followed correctly.

The Mediterranean Lifestyle

The Ten Commandments Of the Mediterranean Diet and Lifestyle

1. Eat a wide variety of fresh, non-processed food.
2. Avoid saturated fat, trans fat, refined sugar, and excess sodium.
3. Substitute olive oil for margarine or butter.
4. Limit portion size.
5. Drink an adequate amount of water.
6. Consume alcohol in moderation.
7. Exercise daily, a minimum of 30 minutes per day.
8. Abstain from smoking.
9. Relax — especially after meals.
10. Laugh, smile, and enjoy life.

The Top Ten Tips for Your Success:

1. Active lifestyle:

The Mediterranean lifestyle encourages one to eat healthy foods, but it also advocates exercise and active lifestyles. At home, you can play with your kids, clean the house or yard, walk with your dog in the park, skate, ride a bike more and drive less, and take the stairs instead of using the elevator. Park your car further from the shopping mall when you go shopping. If possible, walk and take the longer route.

2. Enjoy your meals with family:

Start planning family dinners more often, at least twice a week. Besides having fun moments, your health will also benefit. Don't just pick up fast food to bring home - get your children involved and spend a quality time together cooking a healthy, homemade meal. This will give you a chance to become more creative.

CHAPTER 2

3 Substitute butter with healthy oils:

Always use extra virgin olive oil instead of butter or margarine. If your recipe includes an unhealthy fat, replace it with the same quantity of olive oil. This will be beneficial for your heart; and at the same time, the dish will become even more delicious.

4 Use more spices and herbs and use less salt:

Herbs and spices are rich in antioxidants. They raise the nutritional value of meals and reduce sodium levels. On the other hand, researchers have revealed that salt increases blood pressure. You can use a limited amount of sea salt.

5 Use plant-based recipes:

Meat is the main focus of dishes in the U.S, but the Mediterranean diet encourages using more vegetables. Fruits and vegetables are the core components of this eating pattern, so it's better to put them in the middle of your plate rather than on the side. Choose fruit as dessert. Add some brown sugar or honey to increase flavor. Instead of crackers or chips, eat fresh fruit as a snack.

6 Consume more fish instead of red meat:

The Mediterranean diet recommends eating more fish instead of red meat. Fatty fish like salmon, herring, sardines, or tuna are rich with omega-3 fatty acids and have anti-inflammatory properties.

7 Eat more legumes:

Legumes are a crucial part of the Mediterranean diet. They substitute meat perfectly. Beans are high in minerals and antioxidants and deliver a huge source of protein and fiber.

8 Avoid refined flour and use whole grains:

Avoid white bread and white rice. Try barley, quinoa, or millet.

The Mediterranean Lifestyle

9 Eat seasonal food:

Shop at the local farmers market for fresh seasonal products. Make eating a special ritual and don't let yourself eat in front of the TV or while surfing online.

10 Drink alcohol moderately:

Drink moderately and focus on drinking only red wine. Try not to drink outside of mealtime.

CHAPTER 3

Mediterranean Diet Pyramid

CHAPTER 3

The Mediterranean Diet Pyramid

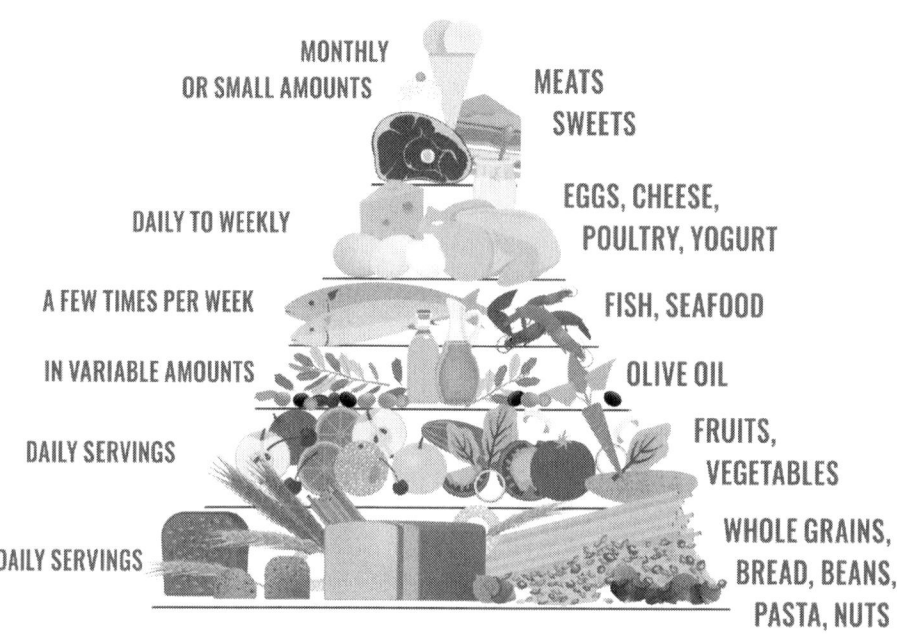

General guidelines of the Mediterranean diet are collected in the Mediterranean Diet Pyramid. It's accepted as the "gold standard" dietary plan that boosts your health. The pyramid was created in 1993 and made the Mediterranean diet popular. The pyramid was developed by Oldways Preservation and Exchange Trust, and Harvard School of Public Health. The pyramid reflects the social and cultural traditions of the Mediterranean lifestyle.

Mediterranean Diet Pyramid

The base of the pyramid showcases the great importance of strong social connection, exercise, and sharing meals with your family and friends. When following the Mediterranean diet, you should prioritize exercises such as running and aerobics, and even small things like walking up the stairs and housework. One of the biggest sections of the Mediterranean Diet Pyramid is devoted to plant-based foods. Fruits and vegetables, beans, whole grains, olive oil, nuts, herbs, and spices are the most important components, so you should consume them daily. Eat fresh and seasonal food and avoid processed foods as much as possible.

Mediterranean Diet Pyramid

1 Whole grains, vegetables, and fruits:

They're an integral part of the Mediterranean diet plan. The grains you should add to your diet should be non-refined whole grains such as quinoa and brown rice. Vegetables can include green leafy vegetables such as kale, spinach, broccoli, Brussels sprouts, cauliflower, and carrots.

2 Olive oil:

Olive oil is a very important part of the Mediterranean diet and is much healthier than other vegetable oils such as canola or sunflower oil. Use olive oil with every dish and replace butter and margarine with olive oil. Consume an average of ½ cup per week.

3 Beans, nuts, and seeds:

Beans, nuts, seeds, and lentils are a great source of protein. Use these ingredients as a substitute for red meat where possible. They provide a more filling, more affordable, and healthier source of protein compared to red meats.

CHAPTER 3

4   Spices:

Use herbs and spices to flavor food instead of sodium-rich table salt. Get creative when flavoring food by combining fresh herbs with olive oil to marinade your food. Season dishes with fresh cracked black pepper for extra spiciness.

5   Fish and seafood:

The omega-3 oils found in fish is required for healthy brain development, and it helps reduce the risk of cardiovascular disease with regular consumption.

6   Poultry, eggs, cheese, and yogurt:

Include poultry, eggs, cheese, and yogurt in your daily diet. Always focus on moderate consumption of any dairy products and monitor their effects on you.

7   Meats:

Red meat should be kept to a minimum, as it isn't the healthiest diet option and can be substituted with legumes, bean, and seeds. When you do eat red meat, try to eat grass fed, organic red meat and keep it to a minimal amount of servings per week.

8   Red wine:

Many studies have shown that one glass of red wine per day can have multiple health benefits. The Mediterranean diet recommends enjoying one glass of red wine. Remember, more than two glasses can be detrimental to your health.

9   Physical activity and social interaction:

The Mediterranean lifestyle includes moderate amounts of daily physical activity and social interaction. Mediterranean's walk or cycle to work and lead very active lifestyles. Meals are also enjoyed as a family and are eaten over

Mediterranean Diet Pyramid

a longer period of time with plenty of conversation and laughs in between. If you can't walk or bike to work, try to take short walks when home and engage in as much physical activity -such as taking the stairs instead of the elevator- during your normal day as possible, Sit down at breakfast, lunch, and dinner and take time to savor your food. Try to taste every bite and identify the ingredients in each bite. Use dinnertime to talk to your family and discuss everyone's day, some goals for the week, your hobbies, and anything interesting you may have seen or heard that day.

The Principles Of The Mediterranean Diet

The principles of the Mediterranean diet are simple and easy to follow. You'll be pleased to discover that the Mediterranean diet is more about what you can and should eat than what you shouldn't eat.

1. Eat a plant-based diet:

Build your meals around vegetables, fresh fruits, beans, and legumes. These whole foods are central to the health benefits of the Mediterranean diet. They provide energy in the form of complex carbohydrates, antioxidants, vitamins, minerals, phytochemicals, and fiber. These nutrient-dense foods fill you up and keep you satisfied, thus helping to control your weight while providing disease-fighting nutrients.

2. Choose whole grains:

Avoid refined grains like white flour and rice. Choose whole grains such as whole wheat, brown rice, oats, barley, corn, quinoa, farro, bulgur, millet, and so on, including whole grain breads, and pasta. Whole grains are higher in nutrients, including minerals, vitamins, and fiber.

CHAPTER 3

3. Eat foods that contain healthy fats, including olives, olive oil, nuts, and seeds:

Olive and olive oil are rich in heart-healthy monounsaturated fats and antioxidants. Add olives and olive oil to your pasta, salads, and stews, and have them as a snack. Nuts and seeds, such as almonds, cashews, pine nuts, hazelnuts, pistachios, pumpkin seeds, sesame seeds, and walnuts are also good sources of healthy fats. Avoid fats that are higher in saturated fats such as butter, cream, lard, or red meat. Completely avoid trans fats such as hydrogenated oils and margarine.

4. Eat fish and seafood:

Eat fish and seafood such as tuna, crab, squid, shrimp, sea bass, sardines, salmon, octopus, mussels, herring, cod, clams, bream, and anchovies.

5. Limit dairy, cheese, and yogurt.

6. Moderation is the key:

It is important to keep portion sizes in check when consuming high calorie and high saturated fat foods like cheese, red meat, refined grains, and foods sweetened with refined sugar.

7. Take time to enjoy life and be physically active:

The Mediterranean way of life is more relaxed than the typical American lifestyle. People in this coastal region take the time to enjoy meals with their families. They walk or bike to work instead of driving, and they take far more vacation time -all of which reduce stress and contribute to good health.

Mediterranean Diet Pyramid

On the Mediterranean diet, you need to consume:

1. At least 4 servings of fresh fruits and vegetables per day.
2. 3 to 5 servings of whole grains per day.
3. 4 to 6 servings of healthy fats per day.
4. At least 3 servings of fish and seafood per week.
5. Up to 7 servings of dairy products per week.
6. Up to one 5-ounce glass of red wine per day for women and two glasses per day for men.
7. 3 to 5 servings (2 eggs) per week.
8. 2 to 5 serving of poultry per week.
9. Up to 4 servings of sweets per week.
10. 3 to 5 servings of red meat per month.

CHAPTER 4

The Benefits of the Mediterranean Diet

CHAPTER 4

The Mediterranean diet offers many health benefits:

1 Weight loss:

For many people who follow it, the Mediterranean diet results in weight loss in a natural and effortless way. While most weight loss diets focus on a strict menu, counting calories, weighing and measuring foods, or undertaking a rigorous exercise program, the Mediterranean diet focuses on enjoying a wide variety of healthy foods and taking the time to savor meals while sharing them with others. By eliminating processed food and fast food from your diet (they are loaded with unhealthy fats, sugar, and chemicals), you significantly lower your caloric intake while eating more food. Without counting fat grams or calories, you trade unhealthy, "empty" foods for those that not only promote good health but also support the loss of stored fat. The Mediterranean diet includes a wide variety of healthful, fresh foods that supply fiber and good fats. Both support weight loss by helping you to feel full. A high-fiber diet also slows the rate at which sugar is absorbed into your bloodstream, which helps control both blood sugar and insulin levels. As insulin triggers fat storage, too much insulin in the bloodstream stops fat loss. Fiber from fruits, whole grains, and vegetables also helps to improve digestion, which can be an important factor in weight loss. Many antioxidants found in fresh fruits and vegetables (such as lutein in apples) can encourage weight loss. Overall, the Mediterranean diet allows people to lose weight naturally and healthfully, without going hungry or eliminating food groups.

https://www.nejm.org/doi/full/10.1056/NEJMoa0708681

2 Improves heart health:

Studies show that healthy monounsaturated fat and omega-3 fat rich Mediterranean diet lowers the risk of heart disease. The following study shows that consuming olive oil can lower the risk of sudden cardiac death by 45% and the risk of cardiac death by 30%.

https://www.ncbi.nlm.nih.gov/pubmed/17058434
https://www.ncbi.nlm.nih.gov/pubmed/23939686

The Benefits of the Mediterranean Diet

3 Helps fight cancer:

A diet that includes lots of fresh vegetables and fruits can prevent cell mutation, lower inflammation, protect DNA from damage, fight cancer, and delay tumor growth.

https://www.ncbi.nlm.nih.gov/pubmed/22644232

4 Prevents and treats diabetes:

Alongside the other benefits, the Mediterranean diet is also an anti-inflammatory diet. This means that the diet can help combat diseases that are caused by inflammation such as metabolic syndrome and type 2 diabetes.

https://www.ncbi.nlm.nih.gov/pubmed/19689829

5 Improve cognitive health and can improve mood:

The Mediterranean diet acts as a natural Alzheimer's and Parkinson's disease treatment because the healthy fats of the Mediterranean diet are good for your brain. Anti-inflammatory fruits, vegetables, and healthy fats like olive oil and nuts are known to fight age-related cognitive decline. They also prevent the harmful effects of free radical damage and toxicity- both of which lower brain function.

https://www.ncbi.nlm.nih.gov/pmc/articles/PMC5538737/
https://www.ncbi.nlm.nih.gov/pubmed/16622828
https://www.ncbi.nlm.nih.gov/pubmed/19262590

CHAPTER 4

6 Strengthen bones:

Olive oil can help your bones stay strong. A study shows that following the Mediterranean diet can help prevent osteoporosis.

https://www.ncbi.nlm.nih.gov/pubmed/24975408
https://www.ncbi.nlm.nih.gov/pubmed/22946650

7 Good for your gut:

Research shows that dieters who follow the Mediterranean diet have a higher percentage of good bacteria in their gut. Research also shows that eating more plant-based foods such as vegetables, fruits, and legumes boost good bacteria production.

https://www.frontiersin.org/articles/10.3389/fnut.2018.00028/full

8 Lowers anxiety and fights depression:

Doctors suggest the Mediterranean diet as a treatment for patients with depression, anxiety, and other mental health issues. Foods such as kale, spinach, and egg contain carotenoids which boost the good bacteria in your gut and improves mood.

https://www.practiceupdate.com/content/healthy-dietary-choices-may-reduce-the-risk-of-depression/74278
https://www.ncbi.nlm.nih.gov/pubmed/29775747

9 Help you live longer:

Following the Mediterranean diet can help you live longer. Studies show that monounsaturated fat is linked with lower levels of inflammatory disease such as cancer, heart disease, depression, cognitive decline, and Alzheimer's disease.

https://www.ahajournals.org/doi/pdf/10.1161/01.cir.99.6.779

10 Good for post-menopausal women:

Menopause can trigger bone and muscle loss. The Mediterranean diet can have a positive impact on bone and muscle loss.

https://www.sciencedaily.com/releases/2018/03/180318144826.htm

CHAPTER 5

Starting the Mediterranean Diet

CHAPTER 5

The Mediterranean diet is a straightforward, easy to follow, and delicious diet, but you need a bit of preparation. Preparing for the Mediterranean diet is largely about preparing yourself for a new way of eating, adjusting your attitude toward food into one of joyful expectation and appreciation of good meals and good company.

Planning Your Mediterranean Diet

There are a few things that you can do to make your transition to the diet easier and more fun.

1. Ease your way into more healthful eating:

Before starting the diet, it can be helpful to spend a week or two cutting back on the least healthful foods that you are currently eating. You might start with fast food or eliminate cream-based sauces and soups. You can start cutting back on processed foods like frozen meals, boxed dinners, and chips. Some other things to start trimming might be sodas, coffee with a lot of sugar, and milk. You should lower butter, and cut out red meats such as lamb, beef, and pork.

2. Start thinking about what you will be eating:

Just like planning for a vacation, you need to plan your diet. Go through the list of foods you need to eat on the Mediterranean diet and get recipe and meal ideas.

3. Gather what you will need:

Everything in the Mediterranean diet is easily found at farmers' markets, grocery stores, and seafood shops. Find out where your local farmers' markets are and spend a leisurely morning checking out what is available. Talk to the farmers about what they harvest and when. Building relationships with those vendors can lead to getting special deals and the best selection. You can join the CSA (Community Supported Agriculture) farm nearby. CSA farms are small farms that sell subscription packages of whatever they are growing that season.

Starting the Mediterranean Diet

For a moderate seasonal or weekly fee, the farm will supply you with enough of that week's harvest to feed your whole family. Freshness is important when following the Mediterranean diet. Joining a CSA is a great way to enjoy the freshness and peak flavor that is so important to the Mediterranean diet. The same is true for your local seafood market and butcher shop. Find out who is selling the freshest, most healthful meats and seafood and buy from them. When you are ready to start, create a shopping list and get as many of your ingredients from your new sources as you can. Two links to find CSA:

> https://www.ifoam.bio/en/community-supported-agriculture-csa
> https://www.localharvest.org/csa/

Here is a link to find local farmers' market in your area (https://www.localharvest.org/)

4 Plan your week:

Planning ahead is essential to success. The diet is heavily plant-based, and you need to load up on fresh fruits, vegetables, and herbs each week. By keeping your pantry stocked with whole grains like whole-wheat pasta, polenta, dried or canned beans and legumes, olive oil, and even some canned, vegetables and fish, you can be sure that you will always have the ingredients for a healthy meal.

CHAPTER 5

5   Adjust your portions:

The idea behind the Mediterranean diet is to make up the bulk of your diet with plant-based foods like fruits, vegetables, whole grains, beans, and nuts. Foods like cheese, meat, and sweets are allowed, but they are consumed only occasionally and in small portions. One way to ensure that you are eating enough plant-based foods while following the Mediterranean diet is to fill half your plate with vegetables and fruit, then fill one-quarter with whole grains, and the last quarter your plate with protein such as beans, fish, shellfish, or poultry. Once every week or two, enjoy a small serving of red meat, such as beef or lamb, or use meat as an accent to add flavor to plant-based stews, sauces, or other dishes. Here are some guidelines that will help you visualize appropriate portions for the Mediterranean diet:

⇨ One ½ cup serving of grains or beans are about the size of the palm of your hand.

⇨ 1 cup of vegetables is as big as a baseball.

⇨ One medium piece of fruit is as big as a tennis ball.

⇨ One 1-ounce serving of cheese is about the size of a pair of dice.

⇨ One 3-ounce portion of meat *(pork, lamb, fish, beef, or poultry)* is roughly the size of a deck of cards.

Starting the Mediterranean Diet

Top Tips for Success

1. Treat yourself like the company:

The Mediterranean diet is as much how you eat as it is about what you eat. The Mediterranean people have a respect for and appreciation of food that inspires them to set a simple, but a beautiful table. Put some flowers on the table; bring out the good china and so on.

2. Learn to savor:

Usually, we eat standing up or while driving to work, watching TV, or finishing up some paperwork. When you are following the Mediterranean diet, you need to turn off the TV, even if you are eating alone. Put away the cell phone, your work, and any other distractions. Enjoy your food even if you are dining alone.

3. Become a social eater:

Gathering around food is something that families and friends do every day in the Mediterranean. Even simple meals are an excuse to invite someone over for good food and conversation. Even when there are no guests, families will linger at the table to talk about the day and enjoy each other's company. Inviting friends and family over for a simple summer lunch or a casual dinner party is a great way to incorporate the Mediterranean approach to dining into your own life.

4. Learn to make substitutions:

Very few things are off-limits in the Mediterranean diet, but moderation is the key. Avoid store-bought products and try to make homemade sauces, dips, soups, chips, and so on.

CHAPTER 5

5. Get some outdoor exercise daily:

Spending time outdoors is just a natural part of any day. Sunshine and good weather abound in the area, as are beautiful scenery and warm oceans. Try to get at least thirty minutes of moderate exercise three times per week – preferably outdoors. Research shows that exercise can help to lose weight, improve cardiovascular health, and improve the overall feeling of happiness and well-being.

6. Don't tempt yourself:

Don't keep food items that are not encouraged on the Mediterranean diet. If you need something to serve guests, the Mediterranean menu offers plenty of choices.

7. Don't overwhelm yourself:

Try not to complicate your life by preparing three weeks' worth of menus at the get-go or trying ten new recipes in a week. Take things slowly and cultivate a relaxed approach to your new way of eating. You don't need a lot of fancy steps to make great meals.

8. Cook your own meals:

Mediterranean dishes are known for being straightforward and easy to prepare. Learn to make a few key dishes and in no time, you will have meals that are much more delicious and better for you than take-out or frozen dinners.

Starting the Mediterranean Diet

9. Don't deprive yourself:

If you love steak, cheese, or chocolate ice cream, don't deprive yourself of it. You can still enjoy your favorite foods in small servings on occasion.

10. Try something new each week:

Eating the Mediterranean way should be fun, exciting, and maybe even a bit exotic. Try to choose one unfamiliar vegetable, fruit, fish, or another ingredient each week. It will keep things interesting and enhance that sense of voyaging to another land.

11. Try growing your own:

The people of the Mediterranean region are very garden-focused. They tend to grow a few food items in their backyards. Growing your own herbs and vegetables is fun, saves money, and is the best way to taste something at its very freshest.

CHAPTER 6

7-Day Meal Planning

CHAPTER 6

Weekly Meal Planner

	Breakfast	Lunch	Dinner	Side dish	Dessert
Sunday	Berry Breakfast Smoothie	Pasta e Fagioli with Orange and Fennel	Stuffed Calamari in Tomato Sauce	Nachos with Toppings	Melon, Plums, and Cherries with Mint and Vanilla
Monday	Mediterra-nean Omelette	Spaghetti al Limone	Provencal Braised Hake	Fava Bean Puree with Chicory	Salted Caramel Panna Cotta Cups
Tuesday	Hearty Berry Breakfast Oats	Spiced Vegetable Couscous	Pan-Roasted Sea Bass	Zucchini Fritters with Yogurt	Dried Fruit Compote

7-Day Meal Planning

	Breakfast	Lunch	Dinner	Side dish	Dessert
Wednesday	Garden Scramble	Moroccan-Style Couscous with Chickpeas	Sage-Stuffed Whole Trout with Roasted Vegetables	Honey and Spice Glazed Carrots	Turkish Stuffed Apricots with Pistachios and Rose Water
Thursday	Scrambled Eggs with Tomato, Spinach, and Ricotta	Spiced Baked Rice with Fennel	Shrimp Paella	Roasted Fennel with Parmesan	Pignoli
Friday	Broccoli Cheddar Egg Muffins	Vegetarian Paella with Green Beans and Chickpeas	Clam Cataplana	Roasted Asparagus with Fingerling Potatoes	Olive Oil-Yogurt Cake
Saturday	Shakshuka	Garlic Prawns with Tomatoes and Basil	Chicken Cacciatore with Wild Mushrooms and Fresh Fennel	Sautéed Cabbage with Parsley and Lemon	Greek Lemon Rice Pudding

CHAPTER 7

Breakfast Recipes

CHAPTER 7

Berry Breakfast Smoothie

Prep time: 2 minutes   **Cook time:** 0 minutes   **Servings:** 1

This smoothie recipe is a great way to enjoy a healthy and filling breakfast during your busy mornings. The Greek yogurt provides a meal's worth of low-fat protein that keeps you going all day.

Ingredients

Vanilla Greek yogurt – ½ cup, low fat
Low-fat milk – ¼ cup
Fresh or frozen blueberries and/or strawberries – ½ cup
Few ice cubes

Method

1. In a blender, place the berries, milk, and yogurt and blend until berries are liquefied.
2. Add the ice cubes and blend on high until smooth.
3. Serve.

Nutritional Facts Per Serving

Calories: 143   **Fat:** 2.9g   **Carb:** 17.6g   **Protein:** 12.7g

Breakfast Recipes

Mediterranean Omelette

Ingredients

Extra virgin olive oil – 2 tsp. divided
Garlic – 1 clove, minced
Red bell pepper – ½, thinly sliced
Yellow bell pepper – ½, thinly sliced
Red onion – ¼ cup, thinly sliced
Chopped fresh basil – 2 tbsp.
Chopped fresh parsley – 2 tbsp. plus extra for garnish
Salt – ½ tsp.
Freshly ground black pepper – ½ tsp.
Egg – 4, beaten

Prep time: 5 minutes   **Cook time:** 12 minutes   **Servings:** 2

Prep your vegetables the night before, and making this omelet will be very easy. Use any vegetables that are in season or need to be used up.

Method

1. Heat 1 tsp. olive in a skillet. Add the onion, peppers, and garlic and stir-fry for 5 minutes.
2. Add salt, pepper, parsley, and basil. Stir-fry for 2 minutes. Remove the cooked mixture from the pan and place on a plate.
3. Heat remaining 1 tsp. olive oil in the same pan and pour in the beaten eggs. Cook until the center is dry and the edges are bubbly, about 3 to 5 minutes.
4. Flip the omelet and spoon the vegetable mixture onto one half of the omelet and fold with a spatula.
5. Place the omelet on to a cutting board.
6. Cut the omelet in half and garnish with fresh parsley.
7. Serve.

Nutritional Facts Per Serving

Calories: 213   **Fat:** 14.9g   **Carb:** 7.8g   **Protein:** 13.7g

CHAPTER 7

Hearty Berry Breakfast Oats

Prep time: 5 minutes   **Cook time:** 20 minutes   **Servings:** 2

Fresh berries and whole-grain oats provide a generous amount of fiber. This combination is not only delicious but nutritious as well. The walnuts supply omega-3 fats and the fresh berries provide vitamin C and other antioxidants.

Ingredients

Whole-grain rolled or quick cooking oats – 1 ½ cups (not instant)
Fresh berries – ¾ cup
Honey – 2 tsp.
Walnut pieces – 2 tbsp.

Method

1. Prepare the whole-grain oats according to the package directions and divide between 2 bowls.
2. Heat the berries and honey in the microwave for 30 seconds.
3. Top each bowl of oatmeal with fruit mixture.
4. Sprinkle the walnuts over the fruit and serve hot.

Nutritional Facts Per Serving

Calories: 212   **Fat:** 6.8g   **Carb:** 33.2g   **Protein:** 6.2g

Breakfast Recipes

Garden Scramble

Ingredients

Extra-virgin olive oil – 1 tsp.
Diced yellow squash – ½ cup
Diced green bell pepper – ½ cup
Diced sweet white onion – ¼ cup
Cherry tomatoes – 6, halved
Chopped fresh basil – 1 tbsp.
Chopped fresh parsley – 1 tbsp.
Salt – ½ tsp.
Freshly ground black pepper – ¼ tsp.
Eggs – 8, beaten

Prep time: 5 minutes   **Cook time:** 12 minutes   **Servings:** 4

Just like a frittata, this savory breakfast dish is a great way to use up small amounts of fresh vegetables. You can use any leftover vegetables in this dish.

Method

1. Heat the oil in a skillet. Add onion, pepper, and squash and stir-fry until onion is translucent, about 3 to 4 minutes.
2. Add parsley, basil, tomatoes, and season with salt and pepper. Sauté for 1 minute.
3. Then pour the beaten eggs over the vegetables.
4. Cover the pan and reduce the heat to low.
5. Cook for 5 to 6 minutes, or until the eggs are cooked through.
6. Slide the frittata onto a platter and cut into wedges.
7. Serve.

Nutritional Facts Per Serving

Calories: 182   **Fat:** 10.4g   **Carb:** 10.9g   **Protein:** 13.1g

CHAPTER 7

Scrambled Eggs with Tomato, Spinach, and Ricotta

Prep time: 5 minutes **Cook time:** 7 minutes **Servings:** 2

You can prepare this delicious Mediterranean scramble breakfast dish with ricotta, tomato, and spinach. This dish is bursting with nutrients, giving you a healthy start to your day.

Ingredients

Extra virgin olive oil – 1 tbsp.
Roma tomato – 1, seeded and diced
Lightly packed baby spinach – 1 cup
Eggs – 3
Egg white – 1
Kosher salt to taste
Part-skim ricotta cheese – 2 tbsp.
Freshly ground black pepper

Method

1. Add the eggs, egg whites, and a pinch of salt in a bowl. Beat the eggs.
2. Heat oil in a skillet. Add the spinach and tomatoes and stir-fry for 3 minutes, or until the spinach is wilted.
3. Add the eggs and cook for 30 seconds. Gently fold. Then add the ricotta and fold the egg mixture. Cook until the eggs are done.
4. Transfer to serving plates. Season with salt and pepper and serve.

Nutritional Facts Per Serving

Calories: 209 **Fat:** 15g **Carb:** 4g **Protein:** 14g

Breakfast Recipes

Broccoli Cheddar Egg Muffins

Prep time: 5 minutes **Cook time:** 14 minutes **Servings:** 6

You can bake these delicious muffins ahead of time. They are a perfect grab and run treat for busy people. Instead of broccoli, you can use zucchini or practically any other vegetable.

Ingredients

Eggs – 8
Egg whites – 4
Dijon mustard – ½ tbsp.
Kosher salt and ground black pepper
Frozen chopped broccoli – 2 cups, thawed
Reduced fat shredded cheddar cheese – ¾ cup
Green onions – 2, sliced
Milk – ¼ cup

Method

1. Preheat the oven to 350F.
2. Spray a muffin tin with cooking spray and set aside.
3. In a bowl, whisk the mustard, eggs, egg whites, 2 tsp. salt, and ½ tsp. pepper. Stir in the broccoli, onions, cheese, and milk. Pour the mixture into the muffin tin.
4. Bake for 12 to 14 minutes or until a knife inserted in the middle comes out clean.
5. Serve.

Nutritional Facts Per Serving

Calories: 169   **Fat:** 10g   **Carb:** 4g   **Protein:** 17g

CHAPTER 7

Shakshuka

Prep time: 5 minutes **Cook time:** 17 minutes **Servings:** 2

Shakshuka is a traditional Mediterranean breakfast dish. An easy to prepare shakshuka recipe of eggs braised in a perfectly spiced sauce of fresh tomatoes and peppers.

Ingredients

Onion – 1, sliced
Garlic – 1 clove, chopped
Chopped tomatoes – 15 oz.
Red bell peppers – 2, chopped
Spicy harissa – 1 tsp.
Olive oil – 2 tbsp.
Chopped parsley – 1 tbsp.
Eggs – 4
Salt and pepper to taste

Method

1. Heat the oil in a skillet over medium heat.
2. Add onions and peppers. Cook for 5 minutes. Stir occasionally.
3. Add garlic and cook for 1 minute more.
4. Add harissa, and tomatoes, and cook for 7 minutes.
5. Season with salt and pepper.
6. Use a wooden spoon to make 4 indentations in the mixture and then add crack an egg to each of the holes.
7. Cover the pot and cook until egg whites are set. Sprinkle with fresh parsley.
8. Serve.

Nutritional Facts Per Serving

Calories: 455　　**Fat:** 38g　　**Carb:** 3g　　**Protein:** 25g

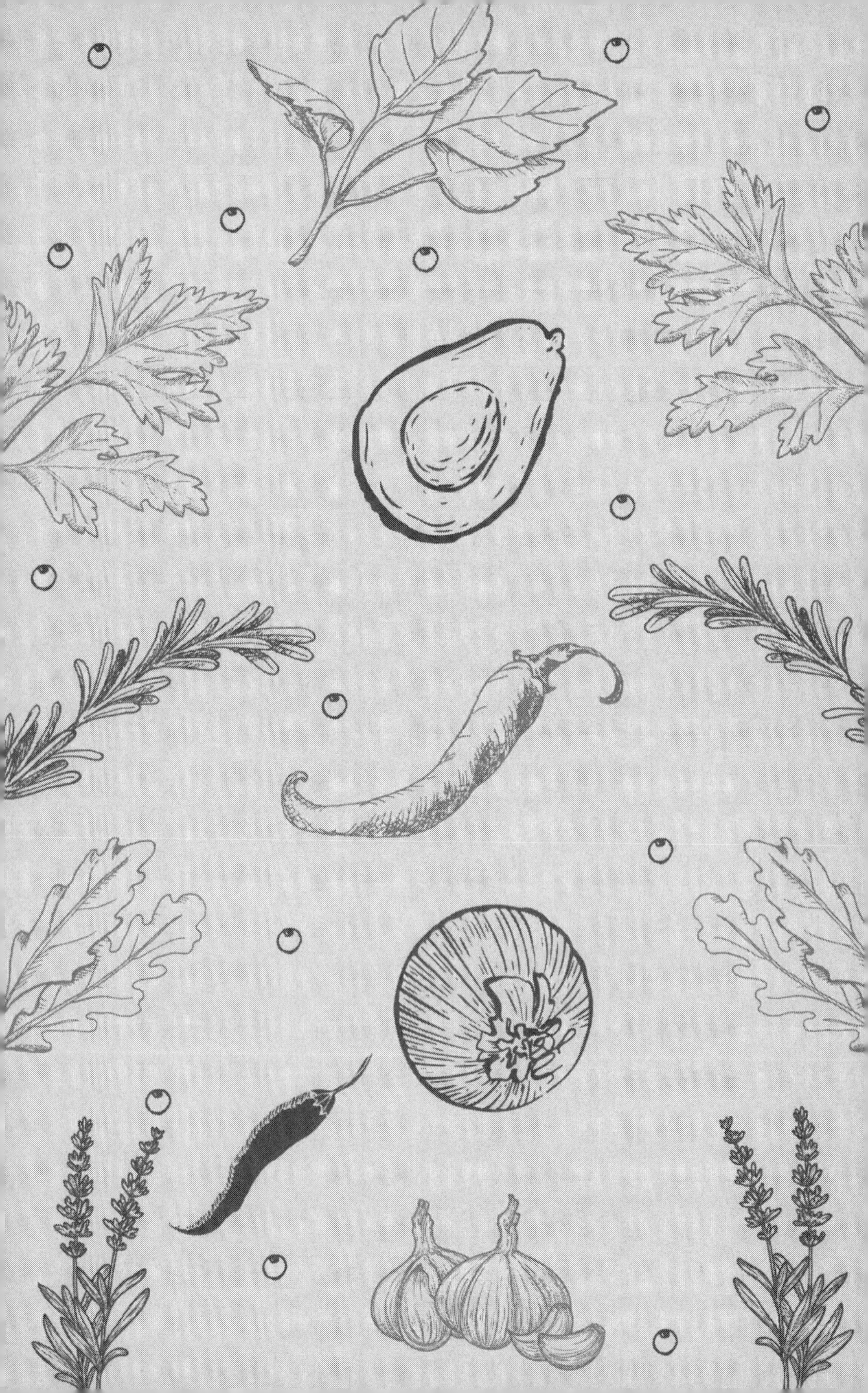

CHAPTER 8

Lunch and dinner

CHAPTER 8

Pasta e Fagioli with Orange and Fennel

Prep time: 10 minutes   **Cook time:** 30 minutes   **Servings:** 5

Ingredients vary according to region to region for this recipe. This pasta gives an Italian flavor with the use of garlic, red pepper flakes, dried oregano, orange zest, and fennel seeds. Using canned cannellini beans can drastically reduce the cooking time. Use small shapes of pasta such as orzo, tubettini, ditalini.

Ingredients

Extra-virgin olive oil – 1 tbsp. plus extra for serving
Pancetta – 2 ounces, chopped fine
Onion – 1, chopped fine
Fennel – 1 bulb, stalks discarded, bulb halved, cored, and chopped fine
Celery – 1 rib, minced
Garlic – 2 cloves, minced
Anchovy fillets – 3, rinsed and minced
Minced fresh oregano – 1 tbsp.
Grated orange zest – 2 tsp.
Fennel seeds – ½ tsp.
Red pepper flakes – ¼ tsp.
Diced tomatoes – 1 (28-ounce) can
Parmesan cheese – 1 rind, plus more for serving
Cannellini beans – 1 (7-ounce) cans, rinsed
Chicken broth – 2 ½ cups
Water – 2 ½ cups
Salt and pepper
Orzo – 1 cup
Minced fresh parsley – ¼ cup

Lunch and dinner

Method

1. Heat oil in a Dutch oven over medium heat. Add pancetta. Stir-fry for 3 to 5 minutes or until beginning to brown.
2. Stir in celery, fennel, and onion and stir-fry until softened (about 5 to 7 minutes).
3. Stir in pepper flakes, fennel seeds, orange zest, oregano, anchovies, and garlic. Cook for 1 minute.
4. Stir in tomatoes and their juice. Stir in Parmesan rind and beans.
5. Bring to a simmer and cook for 10 minutes.
6. Stir in water, broth, and 1 tsp. salt.
7. Increase heat to high and bring to a boil.
8. Stir in pasta and cook for 10 minutes, or until al dente.
9. Remove from heat and discard parmesan rind.
10. Stir in parsley and season with salt and pepper to taste.
11. Drizzle with olive oil and sprinkle with grated parmesan.
12. Serve.

Nutritional Facts for The Entire Recipe

Calories: 502   **Fat:** 8.8g   **Carb:** 72.2g   **Protein:** 34.9g

CHAPTER 8

Spaghetti al Limone

Ingredients

Extra-virgin olive oil – ½ cup
Grated lemon zest – 2 tsp.
Lemon juice – 1/3 cup
Garlic – 1 clove, minced to pate
Salt and pepper
Parmesan cheese – 2 ounces, grated
Spaghetti – 1 pound
Shredded fresh basil – 6 tbsp.

Prep time: 10 minutes **Cook time:** 15 minutes **Servings:** 6

This spaghetti with lemon is a classic Italian dish in which a few ingredients are needed to make a great tasting dish. You only need a few common ingredients such as extra-virgin olive oil, parmesan cheese, pasta, lemon juice, and zest. Adding a little bit of garlic provides depth but doesn't overpower the lemon flavor. Parmesan cheese gives the sauce nutty flavor. Use fresh basil, fresh lemon juice, and high-quality extra-virgin olive oil.

Method

1. In a bowl, whisk garlic, oil, lemon zest, juice, ½ tsp. salt and ¼ tsp. pepper. Stir in parmesan and mix until creamy.
2. Meanwhile, cook pasta according to package directions. Drain, and reserve ½ cup cooking water.
3. Add oil mixture and basil to the pasta and toss to combine.
4. Season with salt and pepper to taste and add cooking water as needed.
5. Serve.

Nutritional Facts for The Entire Recipe

Calories: 398   **Fat:** 20.7g   **Carb:** 42.5g   **Protein:** 11.9g

Lunch and dinner

Spiced Baked Rice with Fennel

Ingredients

Sweet potatoes – 1 ½ pounds, peeled and cut into 1-inch pieces
Extra-virgin olive oil – ¼ cup
Salt and pepper
Fennel – 1 bulb, chopped fine
Small onion – 1, chopped fine
Long-grain white rice – 1 ½ cups, rinsed
Garlic – 4 cloves, minced
Ras el hanout – 2 tsp.
Chicken broth – 2 ¾ cups
Large pitted brine-cured green olives – ¾ cup, halved
Minced fresh cilantro – 2 tbsp.
Lime wedges

Prep time: 10 minutes   **Cook time:** 45 minutes   **Servings:** 8

This hearty rice dish combines several flavorful elements of North African cuisine – fennel, green olives, and sweet potatoes – along with spice blend ras el hanout. The recipe is cooked on the stovetop and ras el hanout is stirred in the rice, so the flavors meld and bloom.

Method

1. Adjust oven rack to middle position and heat oven to 400F. Toss potatoes with ½ tsp. salt and 2 tbsp. oil.
2. Arrange potatoes in a single layer in a rimmed baking sheet and roast for 25 to 30 minutes, or until tender. Stir potatoes halfway through roasting.
3. Remove potatoes from the oven and lower oven temperature to 350F.
4. In a Dutch oven, heat remaining 2 tbsp. oil over medium heat.
5. Add onion and fennel and cook for 5 to 7 minutes, or until softened. Stir in ras el hanout, garlic, and rice. Stir-fry for 3 minutes.
6. Stir in olives and broth and let sit for 10 minutes. Add potatoes to rice and fluff gently with a fork to combine.
7. Season with salt and pepper to taste.
8. Sprinkle with cilantro and serve with lime wedges.

Nutritional Facts for The Entire Recipe

Calories: 207   **Fat:** 8.9g   **Carb:** 29.4g   **Protein:** 3.9g

CHAPTER 8

Spiced Vegetable Couscous

Prep time: 10 minutes   **Cook time:** 20 minutes   **Servings:** 6

Aromatic North African flavors inspire this vegetable couscous dish. For the vegetables, the choices are red bell pepper, zucchini, and cauliflower. The zucchini and bell pepper are sautéed with ras el hanout, garlic, and lemon zest. The marjoram gives it a bit of minty freshness.

Ingredients

Cauliflower – 1 head, cut into 1 –inch florets
Extra-virgin olive oil – 6 tbsp. plus extra for serving
Salt and pepper
Couscous – 1 ½ cups
Zucchini – 1, cut into ½ inch pieces
Red bell pepper – 1, stemmed, seeded, and cut into ½ inch pieces
Garlic – 4 cloves, minced
Ras el hanout – 2 tsp.
Grated lemon zest -1 tsp. plus lemon wedges for serving
Chicken broth – 1 ¾ cups
Minced fresh marjoram – 1 tbsp.

Method

1. In a skillet, heat 2 tbsp. oil over medium heat.
2. Add cauliflowers, ¾ tsp. salt, and ½ tsp. pepper. Mix.
3. Cover and cook for 5 minutes, or until the florets start to brown and edges are just translucent.
4. Remove the lid and cook, stirring for 10 minutes, or until florets turn golden brown. Transfer to a bowl and clean the skillet.
5. Heat 2 tbsp. oil in the skillet.
6. Add couscous. Cook and stir for 3 to 5 minutes, or until grains are just beginning to brown. Transfer to a bowl and clean the skillet.
7. Heat remaining 3 tbsp. oil in the skillet and add bell pepper, zucchini, and ½ tsp. salt. Cook for 6 to 8 minutes, or until tender.
8. Stir in lemon zest, ras el hanout, and garlic. Cook until fragrant (about 30 seconds).
9. Stir in broth and bring to a simmer.
10. Stir in couscous. Cover, remove from the heat, and set aside until tender (about 7 minutes).
11. Add marjoram and cauliflower and gently fluff with a fork to combine.
12. Drizzle with extra oil and season with salt and pepper.
13. Serve with lemon wedges.

Nutritional Facts for The Entire Recipe

Calories: 787   **Fat:** 18.3g   **Carb:** 129.6g   **Protein:** 24.5g

CHAPTER 8

Moroccan-Style Couscous with Chickpeas

Prep time: 5 minutes   **Cook time:** 18 minutes   **Servings:** 6

For this recipe, you need to toast the couscous to boost the flavor. Then sauté the vegetables, toast the spices, add the chickpeas, and add the couscous. The vegetables added in this recipe are pans, onions, and carrots. The spices used are ground anise, ground ginger, and coriander. Garlic, broth, and herbs at the end complete the dish.

Ingredients

Extra-virgin olive oil – ¼ cup, extra for serving
Couscous – 1 ½ cups
Peeled and chopped fine carrots – 2
Chopped fine onion – 1
Salt and pepper
Garlic – 3 cloves, minced
Ground coriander – 1 tsp.
Ground ginger - tsp.
Ground anise seed – ¼ tsp.
Chicken broth – 1 ¾ cups
Chickpeas - 1 (15-ounce) can, rinsed
Frozen peas – 1 ½ cups
Chopped fresh parsley or cilantro – ½ cup
Lemon wedges

Method

1. Heat 2 tbsp. oil in a skillet over medium heat.
2. Add couscous and cook for 3 to 5 minutes, or until just beginning to brown. Transfer to a bowl and clean the skillet.
3. Heat remaining 2 tbsp. oil in the skillet and add onion, carrots, and 1 tsp. salt. Cook for 5 to 7 minutes, or until softened.
4. Stir in anise, ginger, coriander, and garlic. Cook until fragrant (about 30 seconds).
5. Stir in chickpeas and broth and bring to simmer.
6. Stir in couscous and peas. Cover, and remove from the heat. Set aside for 7 minutes, or until the couscous is tender.
7. Add parsley to couscous and fluff with a fork to combine.
8. Drizzle with extra oil and season with salt and pepper.
9. Serve with lemon wedges.

Nutritional Facts for The Entire Recipe

Calories: 649   **Fat:** 14.2g   **Carb:** 102.8g   **Protein:** 30.1g

CHAPTER 8

Vegetarian Paella with Green Beans and Chickpeas

Ingredients

Pinch of saffron
Vegetable broth – 3 cups
Olive oil – 1 tbsp.
Yellow onion – 1 large, diced
Garlic – 4 cloves, sliced
Red bell pepper – 1, diced
Crushed tomatoes – ¾ cup, fresh or canned
Tomato paste – 2 tbsp.
Hot paprika – 1 ½ tsp.
Salt – 1 tsp.
Freshly ground black pepper – ½ tsp.
Green beans – 1 ½ cups, trimmed and halved
Chickpeas – 1 (15-ounce) can, drained and rinsed
Short-grain white rice – 1 cup
Lemon – 1, cut into wedges

Prep time: 10 minutes   **Cook time:** 35 minutes   **Servings:** 4

Paella is a classic Spanish dish. It is cooked with saffron-scented rice with vegetables. The dish is topped with sausage, or seafood or meat. This vegetarian version is made with chickpeas and green beans instead of meat. However, with the rich flavors of tomatoes, garlic, onion, and saffron, you will hardly notice the difference.

Method

1. Mix the saffron threads with 3 tbsp. warm water in a small bowl.
2. In a saucepan, bring the water to a simmer over medium heat. Lower the heat to low and let the broth simmer.
3. Heat the oil in a skillet over medium heat. Add the onion and stir-fry for 5 minutes. Add the bell pepper and garlic and stir-fry for 7 minutes or until pepper is softened. Stir in the saffron-water mixture, salt, pepper, paprika, tomato paste, and tomatoes.
4. Add the rice, chickpeas, and green beans. Add the warm broth and bring to a boil. Lower heat and simmer uncovered for 20 minutes.
5. Serve hot, garnished with lemon wedges.

Nutritional Facts Per Serving

Calories: 709   **Fat:** 12g   **Carb:** 121g   **Protein:** 33g

Lunch and dinner

Garlic Prawns with Tomatoes and Basil

Ingredients

Olive oil – 2 tbsp.
Prawns – 1 ¼ pounds, peeled and deveined
Garlic – 3 cloves, minced
Crushed red pepper flakes – 1/8 tsp.
Dry white wine – ¾ cup
Grape tomatoes – 1 ½ cups
Finely chopped fresh basil – ¼ cup, plus more for garnish
Salt – ¾ tsp.
Ground black pepper – ½ tsp.

Prep time: 10 minutes   **Cook time:** 10 minutes   **Servings:** 4

Garlicky prawn makes a delicious, healthy, and quick Mediterranean-style meal. The traditional Italian prawn dish is usually loaded with butter, but this version uses olive oil. Plump shrimp are tossed in a quick sauce of basil, garlic, white wine, and tomatoes. Serve with the dish with on its own or over polenta, pasta, or alongside roasted potatoes.

Method

1. In a skillet, heat oil over medium-high heat. Add the prawns and cook for 1 minute, or until just cooked through. Transfer to a plate.
2. Add the red pepper flakes, and garlic to the oil in the pan and cook, stirring, for 30 seconds. Stir in the wine and cook until it is reduced by about half.
3. Add the tomatoes and stir-fry until tomatoes begin to break down (about 3 to 4 minutes). Stir in reserved shrimp, salt, pepper, and basil. Cook for 1 to 2 minutes more.
4. Serve garnished with remaining basil.

Nutritional Facts Per Serving

Calories: 282   **Fat:** 10g   **Carb:** 7g   **Protein:** 33g

CHAPTER 8

Stuffed Calamari in Tomato Sauce

Ingredients for the squid
Olive oil – ½ cup, plus 3 tbsp. divided
Large onions - 2, finely chopped
Garlic – 4 cloves, finely chopped
Grated Pecorino Romano – 1 cup, plus ¼ cup, divided
Chopped flat-leaf parsley – ½ cup, plus ¼ cup, divided
Breadcrumbs – 6 cups
Raisins – 1 cup
Large squid tubes – 12, cleaned
Toothpicks – 12

For the tomato sauce
Olive oil – 2 tbsp.
Garlic – 4 cloves, chopped
Crushed tomatoes – 2 (28-ounce) cans
Finely chopped basil – ½ cup
Salt – 1 tsp.
Pepper – 1 tsp.

Prep time: 10 minutes **Cook time:** 25 minutes **Servings:** 6

Quick and easy stuffed squid in tomato sauce is a Sardinian specialty. This version is stuffed with onion, breadcrumbs, Pecorino, garlic, and raisin stuffing that is both savory and sweet.

Method

1. Combine the saffron threads with 2 tbsp. of warm water.
2. In a Dutch oven, heat ½ cup of olive oil. Add the onions and ½ tsp. of salt and stir-fry for 5 minutes. Add the tomato paste and cook for 1 minute more.
3. Add the wine and bring to a boil. Add the fish broth and soaked saffron and bring back to a boil. Lower the heat to low and simmer, uncovered, for 10 minutes.
4. Meanwhile, in a food processor, combine the bread and garlic, and process until ground. Add the remaining ¼ cup olive oil and ½ tsp. salt and pulse just to mix.
5. Add the fish to the pot, cover, and cook until the fish is just cooked through, about 6 minutes. Stir in the sauce. Taste and adjust seasoning.
6. Ladle the stew into the serving bowls.
7. Serve garnished with parsley.

Nutritional Facts Per Serving

Calories: 779 **Fat:** 41g **Carb:** 31g **Protein:** 67g

Lunch and dinner

Provencal Braised Hake

Ingredients

Extra-virgin olive oil – 2 tbsp. plus extra for serving
Onion – 1, halved and sliced thin
Fennel bulb – 1, stalks discarded, bulb halved, cored and sliced thin
Salt and black pepper
Garlic clove – 4, minced
Minced fresh thyme – 1 tsp.
Diced tomatoes – 1 (14.5 ounce) can, drained
Dry white wine – ½ cup
Skinless hake fillets – 4 (4 to 6 ounce) 1 to 1 ½ inches thick
Minced fresh parsley – 2 Tbsp.

Prep time: 10 minutes   **Cook time:** 20 minutes   **Servings:** 4

This tender, moist hake dish is coated in an aromatic, garlicky tomato sauce. Sautéing onions and garlic in olive oil and adding canned tomatoes adds the flavor. Fresh thyme, parsley, and a drizzle of olive oil round out the flavors. Haddock and cod are good substitutes for hake.

Method

1. Heat oil in a skillet over medium heat. Add fennel, onion, and ½ tsp. salt and cook for 5 minutes. Stir in thyme and garlic and cook for 30 seconds. Stir in wine and tomatoes and bring to a simmer.
2. Pat hake dry with paper towels and season with salt and pepper. Place hake into the skillet (skin side down). Spoon some sauce over the top and bring to a simmer.
3. Lower heat to medium-low, cover, and cook for 10 to 12 minutes, or until hake flakes apart when prodded with a knife.
4. Serve hake to individual bowls. Stir parsley into the sauce, and season with salt and pepper to taste.
5. Spoon sauce over hake and drizzle with extra oil.
6. Serve.

Nutritional Facts Per Serving

Calories: 292   **Fat:** 11.1g   **Carb:** 11g   **Protein:** 33g

CHAPTER 8

Pan-Roasted Sea Bass

Ingredients

Skinless sea bass fillets – 4 (4 to 6 ounces) 1 to 1 ½ inches thick
Salt and pepper
Sugar – ½ tsp.
Extra-virgin olive oil – 1 tbsp.
Lemon wedges

Prep time: 5 minutes   **Cook time:** 10 minutes   **Servings:** 4

Roasted fish seems simple, but you need some practice to get it right. To avoid overbaking and getting a dry fillet, this recipe uses a Greek relish. The best way to cook the fish is by pan roasting it on one side, then flip it and finish cooking in the oven. The fish will be well browned, tender, and moist. Cod and snapper are good substitutes for the sea bass.

Method

1. Place the oven rack in the middle and preheat the oven to 425F. Pat sea bass dry with paper towels and season with salt and pepper. On one side of each fillet, sprinkle sugar evenly.
2. In a skillet, heat oil over medium-high. Place sea bass sugared side down in the skillet and cook for 2 minutes, or until browned.
3. Then flip and transfer skillet to oven and roast for 7 to 10 minutes, or until the fish registers 140F.
4. Serve with lemon wedges.

Nutritional Facts Per Serving			
Calories: 225	**Fat:** 4.3g	**Carb:** 1g	**Protein:** 45.5g

Lunch and dinner

Sage-Stuffed Whole Trout with Roasted Vegetables

Ingredients

Red bell peppers – 2, seeded and cut into 1-inch wide strips
Artichoke hearts – 1 (15-ounce) can, drained and cut into quarters
Large red onion – 1, halved and cut into – 1-inch wide wedges
Garlic – 4 cloves, halved
Olive oil – 3 tbsp. divided
Salt – 1 ½ tsp. divided
Ground black pepper – ¾ tsp. divided
Whole rainbow trout – 2, cleaned with hand on
Sage leaves – 3 cups
Juice of ½ lemon

Prep time: 10 minutes **Cook time:** 35 minutes **Servings:** 4

Roasting fish whole makes for a dramatic presentation. Stuffing it with herbs and cooking it atop a bed of roasted vegetables gives it loads of flavor. This recipe uses sage, but you can substitute any herbs including oregano, thyme, or basil.

Method

1. Preheat the oven to 475F.
2. In a baking dish, toss the garlic, onion, artichoke hearts, and bell peppers with 2 tbsp. of the olive oil. Sprinkle with ½ tsp. pepper, and 1 tsp. salt.
3. Roast the vegetables in the preheated oven for 20 minutes. Reduce the heat to 375F.
4. While the vegetables are roasting, prepare the fish. Brush the fish inside and out with the remaining 1 tbsp. olive oil and season with the remaining ½ tsp. salt and ¼ tsp. pepper. Stuff each fish with half of the sage leaves.
5. Remove the vegetables from the oven and place the fish on top. Put back in the oven and bake at 375F for 15 minutes more, or until the fish is cooked through. Remove from the oven. Squeeze the lemon juice over the fish and let rest for 5 minutes.
6. Halve the fish. Spoon roasted vegetables onto 4 serving plates, and serve half a fish alongside each, topped with some of the sage leaves.

Nutritional Facts Per Serving

Calories: 527   **Fat:** 26g   **Carb:** 34g   **Protein:** 45g

CHAPTER 8

Shrimp Paella

Ingredients

Olive oil – 2 tbsp.
Medium onion – 1, diced
Red bell pepper – 1, diced
Garlic – 3 cloves, minced
Pinch of saffron
Hot paprika – ¼ tsp.
Salt – 1 tsp.
Freshly ground black pepper – ½ tsp.
Chicken broth – 3 cups, divided
Short-grain white rice - 1 cup
Peeled and deveined large shrimp – 1 pound
Frozen peas – 1 cup, thawed

Prep time: 10 minutes **Cook time:** 25 minutes **Servings:** 4

Paella is the national dish of Spain. It usually consists of saffron-scented rice cooked with vegetables and topping of sausage, seafood, and other meats. This simplified version includes peas and shrimp. A paella pan is the ideal cooking vessel, but a large cast-iron skillet is a fine substitute.

Method

1. Heat olive oil in a skillet. Add the onion and bell pepper and stir-fry for 6 minutes, or until softened. Add the salt, pepper, paprika, saffron, and garlic and mix. Stir in 2 ½ cups of broth and rice.
2. Bring the mixture to a boil, then lower the heat to low, cover, and simmer until the rice is cooked, about 12 minutes. Scatter the shrimp and peas over the rice and add the remaining ½ cup broth.
3. Place the lid back on the skillet and cook until shrimp are just cooked through (about 5 minutes).
4. Serve.

Nutritional Facts Per Serving

Calories: 409 **Fat:** 10g **Carb:** 51g **Protein:** 25g

Lunch and dinner

Clam Cataplana

Ingredients

Olive oil – 2 tbsp.
Medium red onions – 2, thinly sliced
Minced garlic – 2 cloves
Blub fennel – 1 large, cored and sliced
Portuguese chourico sausage – 6 ounces, diced
Crushed red pepper flakes – ¼ tsp.
Chopped fresh tomatoes – 1 pound
Littleneck clams – 4 pounds
Dry white wine – ½ cup
Chopped flat-leaf parsley – 2 tbsp.

Prep time: 5 minutes   **Cook time:** 25 minutes   **Servings:** 4

Cataplana is a classic Portuguese seafood dish. The dish is often made with a mixture of sausage and shellfish. The dish is cooked in a copper pan also called cataplana. You can use a heavy-bottomed saucepan instead.

Method

1. Heat the olive oil in a large, heavy saucepan over medium heat.
2. Add the fennel, garlic, and onions, and stir-fry for 5 minutes.
3. Add the sausage and stir-fry until vegetables and sausage start to brown, (about 5 minutes).
4. Stir in red pepper flakes and tomatoes and stir-fry for 5 minutes, or until tomatoes begin to break down.
5. Add the clams on top of the vegetables. Add the wine, cover, and cook until most clams have opened (about 8 minutes).
6. Serve the clams in bowls with sausage, vegetables, and broth ladled over them.
7. Garnish with parsley before serving.

Nutritional Facts Per Serving

Calories: 500   **Fat:** 20g   **Carb:** 66g   **Protein:** 12g

Chicken Cacciatore with Wild Mushrooms and Fresh Fennel

Prep time: 10 minutes **Cook time:** 1 hour and 10 minutes **Servings:** 8

The word cacciatore refers to "hunter" in Italian. It means a meat dish braised in a tomato-based sauce with herbs and vegetables. Both fresh and dried wild porcini mushrooms are used frequently in Southern Italian cuisine.

Ingredients

Dried porcini mushrooms – ½ ounce
Boiling water – 1 cup
Olive oil – 2 tbsp.
Boneless, skinless chicken thighs – 12 (about 3 pounds), trimmed of fat
Green bell pepper – 1 large, seeded and cut into rings
Large onion – 1, halved and thinly sliced
Fennel bulb – 1 large, thinly sliced
Garlic – 3 cloves, minced
Minced fresh rosemary – 1 tbsp.
Freshly grated orange zest – 2 tsp.
Fresh thyme leaves – 1 tsp.
Red wine vinegar – 3 tbsp.
Dry white wine – ¾ cup
Tomato paste – 2 tbsp.
Salt – 1 tsp.

Method

1. Preheat the oven to 350F.
2. Soak the porcinis in the boiling water for about 20 minutes.
3. Meanwhile, in a skillet, heat the olive oil over medium-high heat. Add the chicken and brown on all sides. Transfer the chicken to a 9-by-13-inch baking dish as the pieces are browned.
4. Lower the heat to medium. Add the fennel, onion, and pepper and stir-fry for 5 minutes, or until softened. Stir in thyme, orange zest, rosemary, and garlic and stir-fry for 30 seconds. Add the vinegar and cook for 1 minute more. Remove from the heat.
5. Remove the mushrooms from the water and reserve the soaking water. Chop the mushrooms coarsely. Add the chopped mushrooms and the soaking water to the pan along with salt, tomato paste, and wine.
6. Bring to a simmer over medium heat, then add the hot mixture to the baking dish, pouring it over the chicken.
7. Cover with the aluminum foil and bake in the preheated oven for 45 minutes.
8. Remove from the oven and rest for 10 minutes before serving. Serve hot.

Nutritional Facts Per Serving

Calories: 468   **Fat:** 19g   **Carb:** 9g   **Protein:** 58g

CHAPTER 8

Seared Duck Breast with Orange Ouzo Sauce

Ingredients

Duck breast halves – 2
Salt – 1 tsp. plus pinch
Olive oil – 1 tbsp.
Shallot – 1 minced
Thai chile – 1, halved lengthwise
Chopped fennel bulb – ½ cup, plus a handful of the minced fronds for garnish
Ouzo – ¼ cup
Chicken broth – 1 cup
Orange juice – ½ cup
Freshly ground black pepper

Prep time: 10 minutes   **Cook time:** 15 minutes   **Servings:** 4

Ouzo is an anise-flavored liqueur that is popular in both Cyprus and Greece. The anise flavor pairs well with the orange of a Greek spin on the classic French dish Duck a l'Orange. Duck breast is easy to cook but keep it on medium-rare or it will become tough.

Method

1. Sore a cross-hatch pattern into the skin of each duck breast. Sprinkle with salt and set aside for 15 minutes.
2. In a skillet, heat the olive oil and add the duck breasts (skin side down). Cook for 8 to 10 minutes, or until the skin is nicely browned. Turn the breasts over and cook 3 minutes more or until the meat is medium-rare.
3. Remove the breasts from the pan, tent with foil, and let rest for 10 minutes.
4. Meanwhile, make the sauce. In the same skillet, cook the fennel bulb, chili, and shallot for 3 minutes or until vegetables begin to soften.
5. Remove from the heat and add the ouzo. Cook until the liquid is reduced by half.
6. Add the orange juice, broth and salt and bring to a boil. Let the sauce simmer for 5 minutes, or until thickened. Then remove from the heat.
7. Slice the duck breast against the grain into 1/8-inch-thick slices. Arrange the slices onto the 4 serving plates and drizzle the sauce over the top.
8. Garnish with the chopped fennel fronds and serve.

Nutritional Facts Per Serving

Calories: 229   **Fat:** 9g   **Carb:** 7g   **Protein:** 27g

Lunch and dinner

Spice-Rubbed Pork Tenderloin with Fennel, Tomatoes, Olives, and Artichokes

Ingredients

Fennel bulb – 2 large, sliced ½ inch thick
Jarred whole baby artichoke hearts – 2 cups, packed in water, quartered, rinsed, and patted dry
Kalamata olives – ½ cup, halved
Extra-virgin olive oil – 3 tbsp.
Pork tenderloins – 2 (12 to 16 ounce), trimmed
Herbs de Provence – 2 tsp.
Salt and pepper
Cherry tomatoes – 1 pound, halved
Grated lemon zest – 1 tbsp.
Minced fresh parsley – 2 tbsp.

Prep time: 10 minutes   **Cook time:** 30 minutes   **Servings:** 6

The pork tenderloin needs bold seasoning. This recipe uses herbs de Provence to give the pork a distinct flavor profile. You only need 2 tsp. of this herb to season the pork. For vegetables to compliment the pork, the recipe uses cherry tomatoes, Kalamata olives, artichokes, and fennel. You can use jarred whole baby artichoke hearts or frozen ones.

Method

1. Place the oven rack to lower-middle position and preheat oven to 450F. In a bowl, combine 2 tbsp. water and fennel in a bowl. Cover and microwave for 5 minutes, or until soft. Drain and toss with oil, olives, and artichoke hearts.
2. Pat tenderloins dry with paper towels. Season with salt and pepper and sprinkle with herbs de Provence. Spread vegetables in a large roasting pan, then place tenderloins on top.
3. Roast vegetables and pork tenderloins for 25 to 30 minutes, or until pork reaches 145F. Turn the pork once at the halfway mark.
4. Transfer tenderloins to carving board, tent loosely with foil, and rest for 10 minutes.
5. Meanwhile, stir lemon zest and tomatoes into the vegetables and continue to roast until tomatoes have softened (about 10 minutes).
6. Stir in parsley and season with salt and pepper to taste.
7. Slice pork and serve with vegetables.

Nutritional Facts Per Serving

Calories: 452   **Fat:** 14.4g   **Carb:** 37.6g   **Protein:** 49.2g

CHAPTER 8

Flank Steak Peperonata

Prep time: 24 hours   **Cook time:** 20 minutes   **Servings:** 6

Peperonata is an Italian mixture of garlic, tomato, onion, and sweet peppers cooked in olive oil until the peppers are soft and the flavors have combined. This recipe pairs this mixture with flank steak. The steak is marinated for up to 24 hours. To serve, slice the meat into smaller pieces, season the slices with salt and pepper and accumulated meat juices, and arrange the meat with the peperonata. A drizzle of olive oil balances the flavors.

Ingredients

Dried oregano – 2 tsp.
Salt and pepper
Flank steak – 1 (1 ½ pound), trimmed
Extra-virgin olive oil – 1/3 cup, plus 1 tbsp. plus more for serving
Bell peppers – 4, cut crosswise into ¼ inch wide strips
Onion – 1, sliced crosswise into ¼ inch wide strips
Garlic – 6 cloves, lightly crushed and peeled
Diced tomatoes – 1 (14.5 ounces) can
Capers – 2 tbsp. plus 4 tsp. caper brine
Red pepper flakes – 1/8 tsp.
Chopped fresh basil – ½ cup

Lunch and dinner

Method

1. Combine 1 tsp. salt and oregano in a bowl. Cut steak with the grain into 3 equal pieces. Sprinkle steak with oregano-salt mixture and wrap tightly with plastic wrap. Refrigerate for up to 24 hours.
2. In a skillet, heat 1/3 cup oil over medium heat. Add ½ tsp. salt, garlic, onion, and bell peppers. Cover and cook for 10 minutes, or until vegetables are soft. Stirring occasionally.
3. Stir in tomatoes and their juice, pepper flakes, and capers and brine. Cook, uncovered, for 5 minutes. Season with salt and pepper. Transfer peperonata to bowl, cover, and keep warm.
4. Clean the skillet. Pat steaks dry with paper towels and season with pepper. Heat remaining 1 tbsp. oil in the skillet and cook steak 5 to 7 minutes per side, or until meat registers 120 to 125 degrees (for medium-rare).
5. Transfer steaks to a carving board, tent loosely with foil, and rest for 10 minutes.
6. Stir basil into peperonata. Slice steaks and season the slices with salt and pepper. Drizzle with oil.
7. Serve steak with peperonata.

Nutritional Facts Per Serving

Calories: 234   **Fat:** 14g   **Carb:** 14.1g   **Protein:** 15.3g

CHAPTER 8

Lentil Salad with Olives, Mint, and Feta

Ingredients

Salt and pepper
French lentils – 1 cup, picked over and rinsed
Garlic – 5 cloves, lightly crushed and peeled
Bay leaf – 1
Extra-virgin olive oil – 5 tbsp.
White wine vinegar – 3 tbsp.
Pitted Kalamata olives – ½ cup, chopped
Chopped fresh mint – ½ cup
Shallot – 1 large, minced
Feta cheese – 1 ounce, crumbled

Prep time: 1 hour **Cook time:** 1 hour **Servings:** 6

This is a Greek-inspired lentil salad. French green lentils are a good choice for this recipe. Cooking the lentils in the oven heats them gently and uniformly. Salt-soaking helps keep the lentils intact but you can avoid soaking if you don't have time.

Method

1. Add 4 cups warm water and 1 tsp. salt in a bowl. Add lentils and soak at room temperature for 1 hour. Drain well.
2. Place oven rack to middle and heat oven to 325F. Combine lentils, 4 cups water, garlic, bay leaf, and ½ tsp. salt in a saucepan. Cover, transfer saucepan to the oven, and cook for 40 to 60 minutes, or until lentils are tender.
3. Drain lentils well, discarding garlic and bay leaf. In a large bowl, whisk oil and vinegar together. Add shallot, mint, olives, and lentils and toss to combine.
4. Season with salt and pepper to taste.
5. Transfer to a serving dish and sprinkle with feta.
6. Serve.

Nutritional Facts Per Serving

Calories: 249 **Fat:** 14.3g **Carb:** 22.1g **Protein:** 9.5g

Lunch and dinner

Chickpeas with Garlic and Parsley

Ingredients

Extra-virgin olive oil – ¼ cup
Garlic – 4 cloves, sliced thin
Red pepper flakes – 1/8 tsp.
Onion – 1, chopped
Salt and pepper
Chickpeas – 2 (15-ounce) cans, rinsed
Chicken broth – 1 cup
Minced fresh parsley – 2 tbsp.
Lemon juice – 2 tsp.

Prep time: 5 minutes **Cook time:** 20 minutes **Servings:** 6

This is a Greek-inspired lentil salad. French green lentils are a good choice for this recipe. Cooking the lentils in the oven heats them gently and uniformly. Salt-soaking helps keep the lentils intact but you can avoid soaking if you don't have time.

Method

1. In a skillet, add 3 tbsp. oil and cook garlic, and pepper flakes for 3 minutes. Stir in onion and ¼ tsp. salt and cook for 5 to 7 minutes.
2. Stir in chickpeas and broth and bring to a simmer. Lower heat and simmer on low heat for 7 minutes, covered.
3. Uncover, increase heat to high and cook for 3 minutes, or until all liquid has evaporated. Remove from heat and stir in lemon juice and parsley.
4. Season with salt and pepper to taste.
5. Drizzle with 1 tbsp. oil and serve.

Nutritional Facts Per Serving

Calories: 611 **Fat:** 17.6g **Carb:** 89.5g **Protein:** 28.7g

CHAPTER 8

Stewed Chickpeas with Eggplant and Tomatoes

Ingredients

Extra-virgin olive oil – ¼ cup
Onions – 2, chopped
Green bell pepper – 1, chopped fine
Salt and pepper
Garlic – 3 cloves, minced
Minced fresh oregano – 1 tbsp.
Bay leaves – 2
Eggplant – 1 pound, cut into 1-inch pieces
Whole peeled tomatoes – 1, can, drained with juice reserved, chopped
Chickpeas – 2(15-ounce) cans, drained with 1 cup liquid reserved

Prep time: 10 minutes   **Cook time:** 1 hour   **Servings:** 6

This recipe is popular in Greece. Fresh eggplant and dried chickpeas are cooked for hours to create a hearty stew. Firm-tender chickpeas are complemented by the silky texture of the eggplant. The sautéed bell pepper, garlic, onions, oregano, and bay leaves create an aromatic base.

Method

1. Place oven rack on lower-middle position and heat oven to 400F.
2. Heat oil in the Dutch oven.
3. Add bell pepper, onions, ½ tsp. salt, and ¼ tsp. pepper. Stir-fry for 5 minutes.
4. Stir in 1 tsp. oregano, garlic, and bay leaves and cook for 30 seconds.
5. Stir in tomatoes, eggplant, reserved juice, chickpeas, and reserved liquid and bring to a boil. Transfer pot to oven and cook, uncovered, for 45 to 60 minutes. Stirring twice.
6. Discard bay leaves. Stir in remaining 2 tsp. oregano and season with salt and pepper.
7. Serve.

Nutritional Facts Per Serving

Calories: 642   **Fat:** 17.3g   **Carb:** 98.3g   **Protein:** 29.3g

Lunch and dinner

Greek Lemon Rice

Ingredients

Long grain rice – 2 cups, uncooked (soaked in cold water for 20 minutes, then drained)
Extra virgin olive oil – 3 tbsp.
Yellow onion – 1 medium, chopped
Garlic - 1 clove, minced
Orzo pasta – ½ cup
Juice of 2 lemons, plus zest of 1 lemon
Low sodium broth – 2 cups
Pinch salt
Chopped parsley – 1 large handful
Dill weed – 1 tsp.

Prep time: 20 minutes **Cook time:** 45 minutes **Servings:** 6

This recipe could be the best lemon rice recipe you have ever tasted. Loads of flavor from fresh herbs, lemon juice, garlic, and onion. For variation, you can use brown rice. For a gluten-free option, omit the orzo.

Method

1. In a saucepan, heat 3 tbsp. extra virgin olive oil.
2. Add onions and stir-fry for 3 to 4 minutes.
3. Add orzo pasta and garlic and toss to mix.
4. Then stir in the rice and toss to coat.
5. Add broth and lemon juice. Bring to a boil and lower the heat.
6. Cover and cook until the rice is done (about 20 minutes).
7. Remove from the heat. Cover and set aside for 10 minutes.
8. Uncover and stir in lemon zest, dill weed, and parsley.
9. Serve.

Nutritional Facts for The Entire Recipe

Calories: 145   **Fat:** 6.9g   **Carb:** 18.3g   **Protein:** 3.3g

CHAPTER 8

Garlic-Herb Rice

Prep time: 10 minutes   **Cook time:** 30 minutes   **Servings:** 4

Usually, rice is simple and blend. However, this recipe makes a rice dish with deep flavors using only simple ingredients. The recipe uses brown jasmine rice with extra-virgin olive oil. The herbs include basil, parsley, and chives.

Ingredients

Extra-virgin olive oil – ½ cup, divided
Large garlic cloves – 5, minced
Brown jasmine rice – 2 cups
Water – 4 cups
Sea salt – 1 tsp.
Black pepper – 1 tsp.
Chopped fresh chives – 3 tbsp.
Chopped fresh parsley – 2 tbsp.
Chopped fresh basil – 1 tbsp.

Method

1. In a saucepan, add ¼-cup olive oil, garlic, and rice. Stir and heat over medium heat. Add the water, sea salt, and black pepper and mix again.
2. Bring to a boil and lower the heat. Simmer, uncovered, stirring occasionally.
3. Once the water is almost absorbed, add the remaining ¼-cup olive oil, along with basil, parsley, and chives.
4. Stir until the herbs are incorporated and all the water is absorbed.

Nutritional Facts for The Entire Recipe

Calories: 304   **Fat:** 25.8g   **Carb:** 19.3g   **Protein:** 2g

Lunch and dinner

Fresh Bean and Tuna Salad

Ingredients

Shelled (shucked) fresh beans – 2 cups
Bay leaves – 2
Extra-virgin olive oil – 3 tbsp.
Red wine vinegar – 1 tbsp.
Salt and black pepper
Best-quality tuna - 1 (6-ounce) can, packed in olive oil
Salted capers – 1 tbsp. soaked and dried
Finely minced flat-leaf parsley – 2 tbsp.
Red onion – 1, sliced

Prep time: 5 minutes   **Cook time:** 20 minutes   **Servings:** 6

In Tuscany, this hearty salad is a summer favorite. The beans used are fresh borlotti, creamy white beans. But if you don't have fresh shell beans, then dried beans will do just fine. Tuna is the traditional garnish nowadays. Serve this salad Tuscan style, as part of an antipasto, or as a first course for an important meal.

Method

1. Bring a pot of lightly salted water to a rolling boil. Add the beans, bay leaves, and cook for 15 to 20 minutes, or until beans are tender but still firm. Drain, discard aromatics, and transfer to a bowl.
2. Immediately dress the beans with vinegar and oil. Add the salt and black pepper. Mix well and adjust seasoning.
3. Drain the tuna and flake the tuna flesh into the bean salad. Add the parsley and capers. Toss to mix and strew the red onion slices over the top.
4. Serve.

Nutritional Facts Per Serving

Calories: 85   **Fat:** 7.1g   **Carb:** 4.7g   **Protein:** 1.8g

CHAPTER 8

Mediterranean Rice Salad

Prep time: 10 minutes **Cook time:** 25 minutes **Servings:** 4

This is a refreshing salad with incredible flavors. You can use any leftovers you have and serve them alongside the grilled chicken for lunch for the following day.

Ingredients

Extra virgin olive oil – ½ cup, divided
Long-grain brown rice – 1 cup
Water – 2 cups
Fresh lemon juice – ¼ cup
Garlic clove – 1, minced
Minced fresh rosemary – 1 tsp.
Minced fresh mint – 1 tsp.
Belgian endives – 3, chopped
Red bell pepper – 1 medium, chopped
Hothouse cucumber – 1, chopped
Chopped whole green onion – ½ cup
Chopped Kalamata olives – ½ cup
Red pepper flakes – ¼ tsp.
Crumbled feta cheese – ¾ cup
Sea salt and black pepper

Method

1. Heat ¼-cup olive oil, rice, and a pinch of salt in a saucepan over low heat. Stir to coat the rice. Add the water and let simmer until the water is absorbed. Stirring occasionally. Pour the rice into a large bowl and cool.
2. In another bowl, mix together the remaining ¼ cup olive oil, red pepper flakes, olives, green onion, cucumber, bell pepper, endives, mint, rosemary, garlic, and lemon juice.
3. Add the rice to the mixture and toss to combine. Gently mix in the feta cheese.
4. Taste and adjust seasoning.
5. Serve.

Nutritional Facts Per Serving

Calories: 415   **Fat:** 34g   **Carb:** 23.8g   **Protein:** 7g

Lentil and Green Olive Salad

Prep time: 10 minutes   **Cook time:** 30 minutes   **Servings:** 6

Lentils make a delightful salad, especially in early spring or late winter, when the first bitter greens and young onions are sprouting. Dressed with olive oil and lemon juice, lentils have an earthy sweetness that offsets the assertive flavors of early greens and tunas. This can be a protein-rich first course or a main course.

Ingredients

Brown or green lentils – ½ pound
Small onion – 1, peeled
Garlic clove – 1, peeled
Bay leaf – 1
Sea salt and freshly ground black pepper
Pitted green olives – 1 cup, coarsely chopped
Sweet red pepper - 1, cut into long thin strips
Extra virgin olive oil – 1/3 cup
Lemon juice – 3 tbsp.
Bitter greens such as radicchio, chicory, arugula to taste
Zest of ½ lemon
Minced parsley – 1 tbsp.

Lunch and dinner

Method

1. Rinse the lentils under running water. Place in a saucepan over medium heat with 3 cups of water. Add one of the onions, a garlic clove, the bay leaf. Season with salt and pepper and bring to a boil.
2. Lower the heat, cover, and simmer for 30 minutes or until lentils are cooked and tender.
3. When done, drain the lentils. Discard the cooking vegetables and mix while still warm with lemon juice, olive oil, red peppers, and olives. Taste and adjust the seasoning.
4. Garnish and serve.

Nutritional Facts Per Serving

| **Calories:** 269 | **Fat:** 13.5g | **Carb:** 28.4g | **Protein:** 10.7g |

CHAPTER 9

Side dishes and Soups

CHAPTER 9

Nachos with Toppings

Prep time: 15 minutes **Cook time:** 15 minutes **Servings:** 4

This Mediterranean version gives every day nachos a fusion-forward makeover. This recipe swaps out sour cream for Greek yogurt, and tortilla chips for crisped pita triangles. The recipe is compliment with a mint sauce made with Greek yogurt and uses a variety of toppings.

Ingredients for pita chips

Whole wheat pita breads – 8
Olive oil to taste
Salt to taste

Mint sauce

Plain Greek yogurt – 6 oz.
Lemon juice – 2 tsp.
Chopped fresh mint leaves – 1 tbsp.
Olive oil – 1 ½ tsp.

Toppings

Red bell pepper – 1, chopped
Chopped sun-dried tomatoes – ¼ cup
Red onion – ½, chopped
Cucumber, - ½ chopped
Quartered cherry tomatoes – ½ cup
Sliced Kalamata olives – ½ cup
Crumbled feta cheese – ½ cup

Side dishes and soups

Method

1. Heat oven to 400F.
2. Cut the pita bread into quarters and place on an ungreased baking sheet.
3. Sprinkle with salt and drizzle with oil. Mix.
4. Bake until pita chips are crisp and golden brown (about 10 to 15 minutes).
5. Meanwhile, stir together the mint sauce ingredients in a bowl.
6. Divide in servings. Top each serving with toppings and mint sauce.
7. Serve.

Nutritional Facts for The Entire Recipe

Calories: 557 **Fat:** 20.7g **Carb:** 79.6g **Protein:** 20.5g

CHAPTER 9

Zucchini Fritters with Yogurt

Ingredients

Small zucchini – 6, grated
Salt – 1 ¼ tsp. divided
Plain Greek yogurt – 1 cup
Smoked paprika – 2 tsp.
Juice of a ½ lemon
Manchego cheese – 4 ounces, grated
Chopped fresh parsley – ¼ cup
Scallions – 4, sliced
Eggs – 3, beaten
All-purpose flour – ½ cup
Ground black pepper – ¼ tsp.
Neutral-flavored oil (such as sunflower seed, safflower, or grapeseed) for frying

Prep time: 30 minutes **Cook time:** 10 minutes **Servings:** 6

Vegetable fritters are popular throughout the Mediterranean. They get their distinctive Spanish flavor from smoked paprika and Manchego cheese. Using creamy Greek yogurt for the sauce instead of the more traditional mayonnaise or aioli lightens the dish without sacrificing flavor.

Method

1. Sprinkle the grated zucchini with salt and drain for 20 minutes. Then, squeeze out as much as water as possible.
2. Meanwhile, make the yogurt sauce: in a small bowl, stir together the yogurt, lemon juice, smoked paprika, and remaining ¼ tsp. salt.
3. In a bowl, combine the flour, pepper, eggs, scallions, parsley, cheese, and zucchini and stir to mix.
4. Fill a large saucepan with a ½ inch of oil and heat over medium heat.
5. Drop the batter in by rounded tbsp. in the hot oil. Cook 4 to 5 fritters at a time. Flat each dollop with the back of the spoon and cook 2 minutes on each side, or until golden brown. Transfer to paper towels to drain and repeat with the remaining batter.
6. Serve with yogurt sauce.

Nutritional Facts for The Entire Recipe

Calories: 237 **Fat:** 14g **Carb:** 18g **Protein:** 11g

Side dishes and soups

Fava Bean Puree with Chicory

Ingredients

Dried fava beans – ½ pound, soaked in water overnight and drained
Chicory leaves – 1 pound
Olive oil – ¼ cup
Small onion – 1, chopped
Garlic – 1 clove, minced
Salt

Prep time: 5 minutes **Cook time:** 2 hours 10 minutes **Servings:** 6

This is a classic Southern Italian dish. The recipe uses fresh chicory and dried fava beans. The chicory is slightly bitter and crisp when raw but becomes sweet and tender when sautéed.

Method

1. Cover the fava beans in a saucepan with water and bring to a boil. Lower heat and simmer for 2 hours. Drain and mash the beans with a potato masher.
2. Meanwhile, bring a large pot of salted water to boil. Add the chicory and cook for 3 minutes, or until tender. Drain.
3. Heat the olive oil in a medium skillet. Add the onion and pinch of salt. Cook for 5 minutes, or until softened. Add the garlic and stir-fry for 1 minute more.
4. Transfer half of the onion mixture, along with the oil, to the bowl with the mashed beans and stir to mix. Taste and add salt as needed.
5. Serve the puree topped with some of the remaining onions and oil with the chicory leaves on the side.

Nutritional Facts Per Serving

Calories: 336 **Fat:** 14g **Carb:** 40g **Protein:** 17g

CHAPTER 9

Honey and Spice Glazed Carrots

Prep time: 5 minutes   **Cook time:** 5 minutes   **Servings:** 2

This is a simple side dish. Quick-cooked carrots are dressed in a mixture of fresh herbs, vinegar, olive oil, honey, and warm spices. It is an easy and delicious side that is perfect alongside any grilled or roasted fish or meat.

Ingredients

Large carrots – 4, peeled and sliced into ½ inch thick rounds
Ground cinnamon – 1 tsp.
Ground ginger – 1 tsp.
Olive oil – 3 tbsp.
Honey – ½ cup
Red wine vinegar – 1 tbsp.
Chopped flat-leaf parsley – 1 tbsp.
Chopped cilantro – 1 tbsp.
Toasted pine nuts – 2 tbsp.

Method

1. Bring a large saucepan of lightly salted water to a boil and add the carrots. Cover and cook until carrots are just tender (about 5 minutes). Drain and place on a bowl.
2. Add the vinegar, honey, olive oil, ginger, and cinnamon and toss to coat. Add the cilantro and parsley and toss to mix. Garnish with pine nuts.
3. Serve.

Nutritional Facts for The Entire Recipe

Calories: 281   **Fat:** 14g   **Carb:** 43g   **Protein:** 1g

Side dishes and soups

Roasted Fennel with Parmesan

Prep time: 5 minutes **Cook time:** 30 minutes **Servings:** 4

Fresh fennel is used widely in the Mediterranean dishes. It has a crisp texture when eaten raw and has a light licorice flavor. When roasted or sautéed, it becomes sweet and beautifully caramelized. Paired with toasted Parmesan cheese, this is a delightful dish.

Ingredients

Fennel bulbs – 2 pounds, cored and cut into 8 wedges each, keep fronds for garnish
Olive oil – ¼ cup
Salt and black pepper
Red pepper flakes – 1 ¼ tsp.
Freshly grated Parmesan cheese – ½ cup

Method

1. Preheat the oven to 350F.
2. Arrange the fennel wedges on a large, rimmed baking sheet and drizzle with oil.
3. Season with salt, black pepper, and red pepper flakes. Sprinkle the cheese over the top.
4. Bake in the preheated oven until the fennel is tender and cheese is golden brown (about 30 minutes). Remove from the oven and let cool in the oil until just warm.
5. Transfer to plates and garnish with reserved fennel fronds.

Nutritional Facts for The Entire Recipe

Calories: 237 **Fat:** 19g **Carb:** 10g **Protein:** 11g

CHAPTER 9

Roasted Asparagus with Fingerling Potatoes

Prep time: 5 minutes   **Cook time:** 20 minutes   **Servings:** 4

Roasted asparagus concentrates its natural sweetness. The thinly sliced roasted potato gets a golden-brown color, which is creamy in the middle and crisp on the outside. Together, they are divine!

Ingredients

Asparagus – 1 pound, trimmed
Fingerling potatoes – 1 pound, cut into thin rounds
Scallions – 2, thinly sliced
Olive oil – 3 tbsp.
Salt – ¾ tsp.
Freshly ground black pepper – ¼ tsp.
Fresh thyme leaves – 1 tbsp.

Method

1. Preheat the oven to 450F.
2. In a baking dish, combine scallions, potatoes, and asparagus and toss to mix. Add salt, pepper, and olive oil and toss again to coat well.
3. Spread the vegetables out in a thin layer and roast in the preheated oven for 20 minutes, (stirring once) or until the vegetables are tender.
4. Sprinkle with thyme leaves before serving. Serve.

Nutritional Facts for The Entire Recipe

Calories: 197   **Fat:** 11g   **Carb:** 24g   **Protein:** 5g

Side dishes and soups

Sautéed Cabbage with Parsley and Lemon

Ingredients

Green cabbage – 1 ¼ pounds, cored and sliced thin
Extra-virgin olive oil – 2 tbsp.
Onion – 1, halved, and sliced thin
Salt and pepper
Chopped fresh parsley – ¼ cup
Lemon juice – 1 ½ tsp.

Prep time: 5 minutes   **Cook time:** 15 minutes   **Servings:** 6

This recipe aims to use green cabbage and bring out the vegetable's natural sweetness while maintaining their crisp-tender texture. The recipe pan-steams and sautées the cabbage instead of boiling or braising it. A precooking step of soaking the cabbage lowers bitterness and preserves extra moisture. Lemon juice provides a punch and cooked onion helps to reinforce sweetness.

Method

1. In a bowl, place the cabbage and cover with cold water. Let sit for 3 minutes then drain.
2. In a skillet, heat 1 tbsp. oil. Add ¼ tsp. salt and onion and cook for 5 to 7 minutes, or until lightly browned. Transfer to a bowl.
3. Add the remaining 1 tbsp. oil in the skillet. Add cabbage, ½ tsp. salt, and ¼ tsp. pepper. Cover and cook, without stirring for 3 minutes or until cabbage is wilted. Stir and continue to cook, uncovered for 4 minutes, or until cabbage is crisp-tender. Stir twice.
4. Remove from heat, stir in parsley, onion, and lemon juice. Season with salt and pepper and serve.

Nutritional Facts Per Serving

Calories: 73   **Fat:** 4.9g   **Carb:** 7.6g   **Protein:** 1.5g

CHAPTER 9

Root Vegetable Soup with Garlic Aioli

Ingredients for the soup

Vegetable broth – 8 cups
Salt – ½ tsp.
Leek – 1, chopped
Carrots – 1 pound, peeled and diced
Potatoes – 1 pound, peeled and diced
Turnips – 1 pound, peeled and chopped
Red bell pepper – 1, cut into strips
Fresh oregano – 2 tbsp.

For the aioli

Garlic – 5 cloves, minced
Salt – ¼ tsp.
Olive oil – 2/3 cup
Lemon juice – 1 drop

Prep time: 10 minutes   **Cook time:** 25 minutes   **Servings:** 4

This vegetable soup is simple. The ingredients are accessible and humble, but the finished dish is far more than the sum of its parts. The broth takes on the vegetables earthy flavors as the vegetables become meltingly tender. The garlicky aioli dissolves into the soup giving it more flavor and richness.

Method

1. Bring the broth and salt to a boil. One by one, add the vegetables. Add the carrots first, then leeks, potatoes, turnips, and finely red bell peppers. Boil the vegetables for about 8 minutes or until soft.
2. Meanwhile, make the aioli. Grind the garlic to a paste and mix with the salt. Continue to whisk and add the olive oil in a thin stream. Continue to whisk and add the lemon juice.
3. Serve the vegetables in the broth. Dolloped with the aioli and garnished with the fresh oregano.

Nutritional Facts Per Serving

Calories: 559   **Fat:** 37g   **Carb:** 46g   **Protein:** 15g

Side dishes and soups

Classic Gazpacho

Ingredients

Cubed day-old whole-wheat bread - 2 cups
Garlic – 2 cloves
Salt – 2 tsp.
Ripe tomatoes – 2 pounds, seeded
Cucumber – 1 medium, peeled and seeded
Green bell pepper – ¼, seeded
Sherry vinegar – 1 tbsp.
Olive oil – ½ cup, plus more for garnish
Black pepper for garnish

Prep time: 10 minutes   **Cook time:** 0 minutes   **Servings:** 4

This is classic gazpacho – a chilled soup made with ripe summer tomatoes and cucumber. It is thickened with bread and spiked with sherry vinegar. The soup is refreshing for a perfect for a warm day. You can substitute sherry vinegar with red wine vinegar.

Method

1. Soak the bread in water for 10 minutes. Drain and squeeze out the excess water.
2. Meanwhile, bring a small pot of water to a boil. Add the garlic and simmer for 2 to 3 minutes. Remove the garlic and discard the water.
3. In a blender, combine vinegar, bell pepper, cucumber, tomatoes, salt, soaked bread, and garlic. Process until smooth.
4. Keep the blender running and add a ½ cup of the olive oil in a thin stream.
5. Process until the soup is emulsified. Taste and adjust seasoning as needed.
6. Cover and refrigerate the soup for at least 3 hours or until chilled completely.
7. Garnish with olive oil and freshly ground black pepper and serve chilled.

Nutritional Facts Per Serving

Calories: 447   **Fat:** 28g   **Carb:** 42g   **Protein:** 12g

CHAPTER 9

White Bean Dip with Garlic and Rosemary

Prep time: 5 minutes **Cook time:** 0 minutes **Makes:** 1 ¼ cups

White beans are a common ingredient in the Mediterranean diet. Processing the beans with olive oil produces a buttery, creamy quality dip. This dip also combines cayenne, garlic, rosemary, and lemon. You can serve this dip with toasted baguette, pita chips or raw vegetables.

Ingredients

Cannellini beans – 1 (15-ounce) can, rinsed
Extra-virgin olive oil – ¼ cup
Water – 2 tbsp.
Lemon juice – 2 tsp.
Minced fresh rosemary - 1 tsp.
Minced garlic clove – 1
Salt and pepper to taste
Pinch cayenne pepper

Method

1. In a food processor, process beans, garlic, rosemary, lemon juice, water, 3 tbsp. oil, ¼ tsp. salt, ¼ tsp. pepper, and cayenne until smooth (about 45 seconds).

2. Transfer to a serving bowl and cover with plastic wrap. Set aside for 30 minutes so flavors meld.

3. Season with salt and pepper and drizzle with the remaining oil before serving.

Nutritional Facts for The Entire Recipe

Calories: 1859 **Fat:** 54.2g **Carb:** 257.2g **Protein:** 100.6g

Side dishes and soups

Spicy Feta and Roasted Red Pepper Dip

Prep time: 5 minutes **Cook time:** 0 minutes **Servings:** 2 cups

For this dip, feta cheese is processed with roasted red peppers to make a light, but rich dip. Usage of cayenne pepper gives this dip the necessary heat, but if you like, you can reduce the cayenne to ¼ for a less spicy version. Serve this dip with raw vegetables, fresh warm pita, or pita chips

Ingredients

Feta cheese – 8 ounces, crumbled
Jarred roasted red peppers – 1 cup, rinsed, patted, dry, and chopped
Extra-virgin olive oil – 1/3 cup, plus extra for serving
Lemon juice – 1 tbsp.
Cayenne pepper – ½ tsp.
Pepper – ¼ tsp.

Method

1. In a food processor, process the pepper, cayenne, lemon juice, oil, red peppers, and feta until smooth.
2. Transfer mixture to a bowl and drizzle with oil to taste.
3. Serve.

Nutritional Facts for The Entire Recipe

Calories: 1208   **Fat:** 115.8g   **Carb:** 14.5g   **Protein:** 33.5g

CHAPTER 10

Desserts

CHAPTER 10

Melon, Plums, and Cherries with Mint and Vanilla

Prep time: 5 minutes　　**Cook time:** 0 minutes　　**Servings:** 6

Fresh fruit salad is a great Mediterranean dessert, breakfast, or mid-afternoon snack. A combination of cherries, plums, and cantaloupe offers a range of complementary flavors and the recipe also looks beautiful. Mashing the mint and sugar together works perfectly, balancing the flavors. The balance of fresh basil, mint, and pepper makes the recipe appealing.

Ingredients

Sugar – 4 tsp.
Minced fresh mint – 1 Tbsp.
Cantaloupe – 3 cups, cut into ½ pieces
Plums - 2 halved, pitted, and cut into 1/2-inch pieces
Fresh sweet cherries – 8 ounces, pitted and halved
Vanilla extract – ¼ tsp.
Lime juice – 1 Tbsp. plus extra for seasoning

Method

1. In a bowl, combine the mint and sugar. Press mixture with a spatula for 30 seconds or until the sugar becomes damp. Add vanilla, cherries, plums, and cantaloupe and gently toss to combine.
2. Let the mixture sit at room temperature for 15 to 30 minutes or until the fruits release their juices. Stir occasionally.
3. Stir in lemon juice and season with extra lime juice to taste.
4. Serve.

Nutritional Facts Per Serving

Calories: 93　　**Fat:** 0.3g　　**Carb:** 23g　　**Protein:** 1g

Desserts

Dried Fruit Compote

Ingredients

Water – 4 cups
Honey – 3 tbsp.
Lemon zest – 2 strips, plus 1 Tbsp. juice
Cinnamon sticks – 2
Ground coriander – 1 ¼ tsp.
Dried Turkish or Calimyrna figs – 2 cups, stemmed
Dried apricots – ¾ cup
Dried cherries – ½ cup

Prep time: 10 minutes   **Cook time:** 50 minutes   **Servings:** 6

This recipe is a delicately spiced, naturally sweet dried fruit dessert recipe. It includes tangy cherries, supple apricots, and succulent figs. As the fruits are cooked, they become plump and tender and create a lush flavorful sauce. Serve the compote warm or chilled.

Method

1. In a saucepan, bring honey, water, lemon zest, juice, cinnamon sticks and coriander to a boil. Cook, stirring occasionally, until the honey has dissolved (about 2 minutes).
2. Stir in apricots and figs and return to boil. Lower heat to medium-low simmer for 30 minutes, or until fruit is plump and tender. Stir occasionally.
3. Stir in cherries and cook for 15 to 20 minutes more, or until cherries are plump and tender.
4. Remove from heat. Discard lemon zest and cinnamon sticks and cool the mixture slightly.
5. Serve warm.

Nutritional Facts Per Serving

Calories: 215   **Fat:** 1g   **Carb:** 55.5g   **Protein:** 2.5g

CHAPTER 10

Salted Caramel Panna Cotta Cups

Prep time: 5 minutes   **Cook time:** 10 minutes   **Servings:** 4

This panna cotta dessert recipe is really easy to make. The cream is flavored with vanilla and sugar. The salted caramel is chilled and then the sugar and vanilla is poured over. This method creates a recipe that has 3 layers. The delicate yet simple mix of smooth runny caramel and wobbly panna cotta will impress your guests.

Ingredients

Salted caramel sauce – ½ cup
Whole milk – 1 ½ cups
Powdered gelatin – 2 ½ tsp.
Caster sugar – 1/3 cup
Heavy cream – 1 ½ cups
Pure vanilla extract – 1 tsp.
Sea salt – 1 pinch

Desserts

Method

1. Divide the caramel sauce between four dessert glasses.
2. Keep the glasses in the refrigerator to chill.
3. In a saucepan, pour milk and sprinkle with gelatin. Set aside for 5 minutes.
4. Place the pan over very low heat and heat for 2 minutes. Stir frequently. Your aim is to get the milk warm enough to make the gelatin melt.
5. Add the caster sugar once the gelatin has dissolved.
6. Remove from heat once the sugar has dissolved. Stir in the salt, vanilla, and cream.
7. Pour the mixture over the cold caramel. Keep in the refrigerator for 3 hours or until set.
8. Serve.

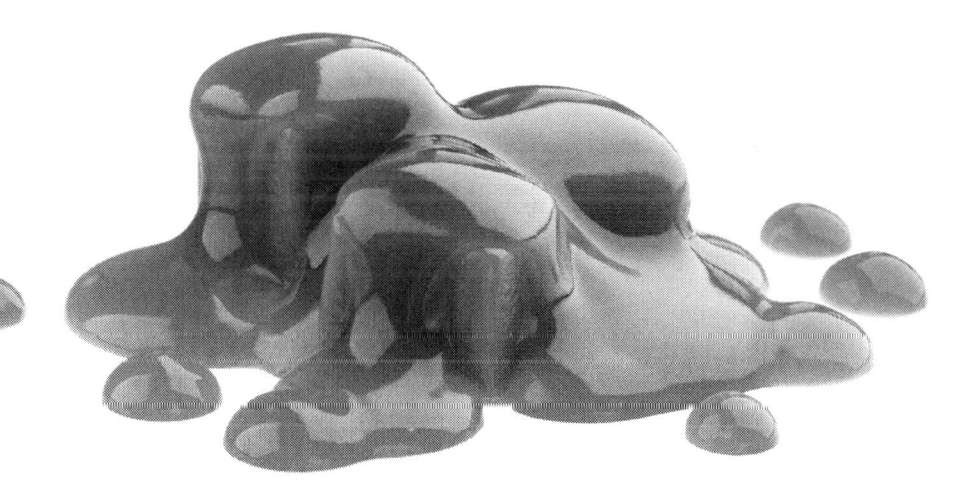

Nutritional Facts Per Serving

Calories: 510   **Fat:** 36g   **Carb:** 42g   **Protein:** 7g

CHAPTER 10

Greek Lemon Rice Pudding

Ingredients

Water – 2 cups
Arborio rice – 1 cup
Salt – ½ tsp.
Vanilla bean – 1
Whole milk – 4 ½ cups, plus extra as needed
Sugar – ½ cup
Cinnamon – ½ stick
Bay leaves – 2
Grated lemon zest – 2 tsp.

Prep time: 10 minutes **Cook time:** 1 hour **Servings:** 8

This recipe creates a Greek rice pudding that has a thick, velvety-smooth texture. Because of the short ingredients list, balance is the key. The rice is cooked, then added to whole milk to make the pudding. Bay leaves offer a balanced floral note.

Method

1. In a saucepan, bring water to boil over medium-high heat. Stir in rice and salt. Reduce heat to low, cover, and simmer for 15 to 20 minutes, or until water is almost fully absorbed.
2. Cut vanilla bean and stir vanilla beans and seeds, milk, sugar, cinnamon stick, and bay leaves into the rice. Cook, uncovered, stirring often for 35 to 45 minutes, or until the pudding has thickened.
3. Turn off heat and discard bay leaves, cinnamon stick, and vanilla bean. Stir in lemon zest. Transfer pudding to a large bowl and cool completely.
4. Serve.

Nutritional Facts Per Serving

Calories: 191 **Fat:** 3.1g **Carb:** 36.9g **Protein:** 4.5g

Desserts

Turkish Stuffed Apricots with Pistachios and Rose Water

Ingredients

Plain Greek yogurt – ½ cup
Sugar – ¼ cup
Rose water – ½ tsp.
Grated lemon zest – ½ tsp. plus 1 tbsp. juice
Salt
Water – 2 cups
Green cardamom pods – 4, cracked
Bay leaves – 2
Whole dried apricots – 24
Shelled pistachios – ¼ cup, toasted and chopped fine

Prep time: 5minutes **Cook time:** 35 minutes **Servings:** 6

Stuffed apricots are an iconic Turkish dessert. This recipe tweaked the sugar concentration of the sugary syrup to quicken the cook time. Cardamom pods and bay leaves add an aromatic depth to the fruit. Thick Greek yogurt, buffalo cream, and rose water enhance the floral qualities of the apricots. Chopped toasted pistachios contribute to a beautiful finish.

Method

1. In a bowl, combine salt, lemon zest, rose water, 1 tsp. sugar and yogurt. Keep in the refrigerator until ready to use.
2. In a saucepan, bring water, bay leaves, cardamom pods, lemon juice, and remaining sugar to a simmer. Cook until sugar dissolved, about 2 minutes. Stirring occasionally.
3. Stir in apricots, return to simmer, and cook, occasionally stirring, until plump and tender, about 25 to 30 minutes — transfer apricots to a plate.
4. Discard bay leaves and cardamom pods. Bring syrup to a boil and cook for 4 to 6 minutes, or until thickened to 3 tbsp. Let cool.
5. Place pistachios in a shallow bowl. Pipe filling evenly into the opening of each apricot and dip exposed filling into pistachios.
6. Drizzle apricots with syrup and serve.

Nutritional Facts Per Serving

Calories: 141 **Fat:** 3.5g **Carb:** 27.9g **Protein:** 3.2g

CHAPTER 10

Pignoli

Ingredients

Slivered almonds – 1 2/3 cups
Sugar – 1 1/3 cups
Large egg whites – 2
Pine nuts – 1 cup

Prep time: 10 minutes   **Cook time:** 15 minutes   **Servings:** 20

With a nutty flavor profile and a light texture from egg whites, the classic southern Italian cookies known as pignoli need only a few ingredients and are very simple to make. For the base, the recipe uses slivered almonds with granulated sugar. The base is easy enough to roll. Then they are coated with pine nuts.

Method

1. Place the oven racks to upper-middle and lower-middle positions. Preheat the oven to 375F. Line 2 baking sheets with parchment paper.
2. Process sugar and almonds in a food processor until finely ground. Add egg whites and process until smooth. Transfer to a bowl and place pine nuts in a shallow bowl.
3. Working 1 scant tbsp. dough at a time, roll into balls. Roll in pine nuts to coat and space 2 inches apart on preheated sheets.
4. Bake cookies for 13 to 15 minutes. Switch and rotate sheets halfway through baking. Let cookies cool and serve.

Nutritional Facts Per Serving

Calories: 328   **Fat:** 15.7g   **Carb:** 46.3g   **Protein:** 5.9g

Desserts

Olive Oil- Yogurt Cake

Ingredients for the cake

All-purpose flour – 3 cups
Baking powder – 1 tbsp.
Salt – 1 tsp.
Granulated sugar – 1 ¼ cups
Large eggs – 4
Extra-virgin olive oil – 1 ¼ cups
Plain whole-milk yogurt – 1 cup

Lemon glaze

Lemon juice – 2 to 3 tbsp.
Plain whole-milk yogurt – 1 tbsp.
Confectioners' sugar – 2 cups

Prep time: 10 minutes   **Cook time:** 45 minutes   **Servings:** 12

This cake is popular in Spain and France and exists in many forms. The cake can be baked in a bundt pan, loaf pan, baking dish, or cake pan but the basic recipe is the same: yogurt and extra virgin olive oil are combined with flour, sugar, eggs, and leavener to create a moist, delicate cake with a slightly coarse crumb and a subtly tangy, mildly fruity aroma.

Method

1. Place the oven rack to low position and preheat the oven to 350F. Grease a 12-cup nonstick Bundt pan. In a bowl, whisk salt, baking powder, and flour. In another bowl, whisk eggs and sugar until sugar mostly dissolved, about 1 minute. Whisk in yogurt and oil and mix until combined. Stir in flour mixture until combined and no dry flour remains.
2. Pour batter into prepared pan and smooth the top. Bake for 40 to 45 minutes, or until cake is golden brown and wooden skewer inserted into the center comes out clean. Rotate pan halfway through baking.
3. To make the lemon glaze: in a bowl, whisk confectioners' sugar, yogurt, and 2 tbsp. lemon juice. Add more lemon juice gradually as needed. Let cook cool for 10 minutes then drizzle half of the glaze over warm cake and cool for 1 hour. Drizzle remaining glaze over cake and let cool completely.

Nutritional Facts Per Serving

Calories: 844   **Fat:** 48.8g   **Carb:** 104.7g   **Protein:** 6g

Conclusion

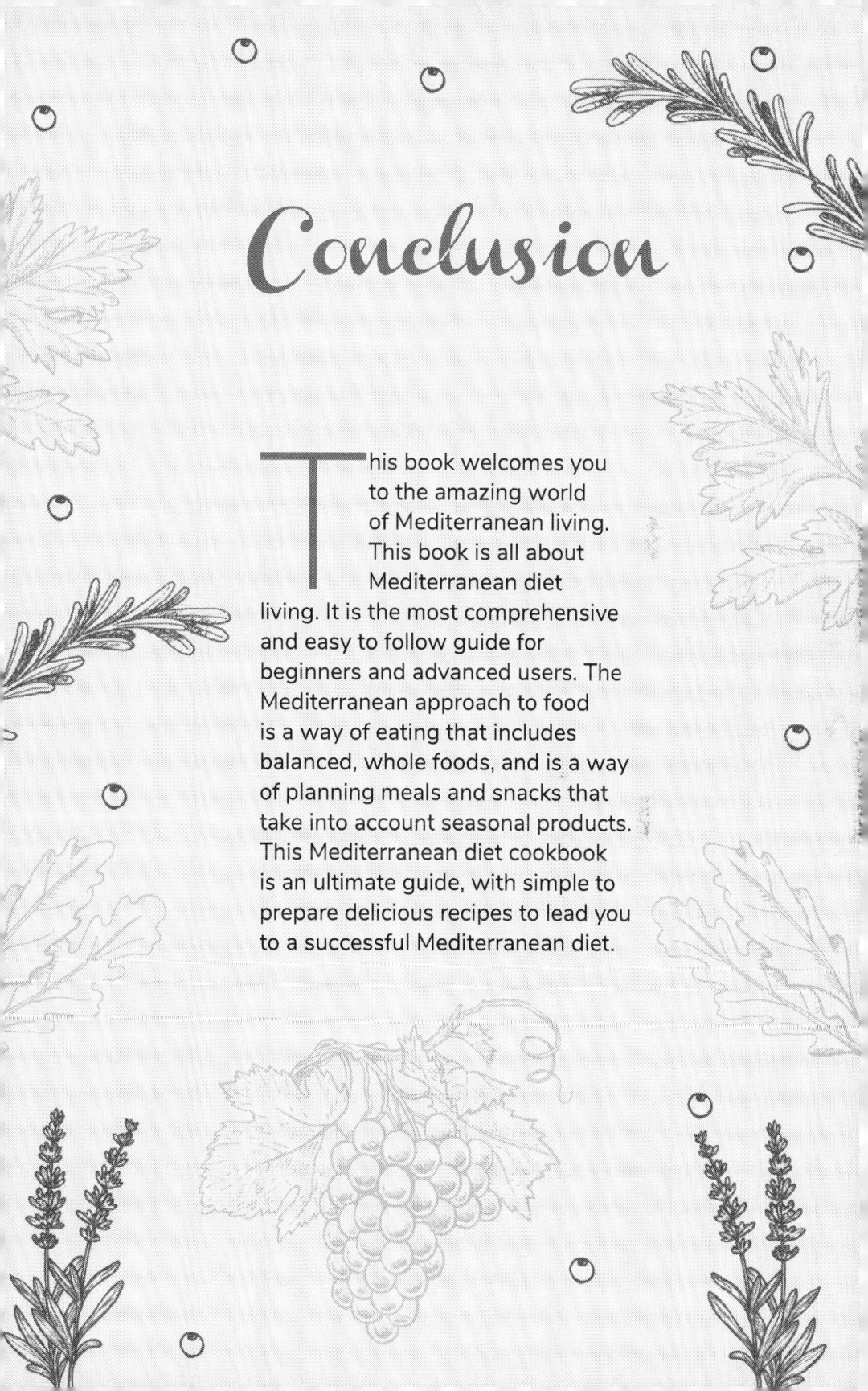

This book welcomes you to the amazing world of Mediterranean living. This book is all about Mediterranean diet living. It is the most comprehensive and easy to follow guide for beginners and advanced users. The Mediterranean approach to food is a way of eating that includes balanced, whole foods, and is a way of planning meals and snacks that take into account seasonal products. This Mediterranean diet cookbook is an ultimate guide, with simple to prepare delicious recipes to lead you to a successful Mediterranean diet.

Index

B
Berry Breakfast Smoothie 44
Broccoli Cheddar Egg Muffins 49

C
Chicken Cacciatore with Wild Mushrooms and Fresh Fennel 70
Chickpeas with Garlic and Parsley 77
Clam Cataplana 69
Classic Gazpacho 97

D
Dried Fruit Compote 103

F
Fava Bean Puree with Chicory 91
Flank Steak Peperonata 74
Fresh Bean and Tuna Salad 81

G
Garden Scramble 47
Garlic Prawns with Tomatoes and Basil 63
Garlic-Herb Rice 80
Greek Lemon Rice Pudding 106
Greek Lemon Rice 79

H
Hearty Berry Breakfast Oats 46
Honey and Spice Glazed Carrots 92

L
Lentil and Green Olive Salad 84
Lentil Salad with Olives, Mint, and Feta 76

M
Mediterranean Omelette 45
Mediterranean Rice Salad 82
Melon, Plums, and Cherries with Mint and Vanilla 102
Moroccan-Style Couscous with Chickpeas 60

N
Nachos with Toppings 88

O
Olive Oil- Yogurt Cake 109

P
Pan-Roasted Sea Bass 66
Pasta e Fagioli with Orange and Fennel 54
Pignoli 108
Provencal Braised Hake 65

R
Roasted Asparagus with Fingerling Potatoes 94
Roasted Fennel with Parmesan 93
Root Vegetable Soup with Garlic Aioli 96

S
Sage-Stuffed Whole Trout with Roasted Vegetables 67
Salted Caramel Panna Cotta Cups 104
Sautéed Cabbage with Parsley and Lemon 95
Scrambled Eggs with Tomato, Spinach, and Ricotta 48
Seared Duck Breast with Orange Ouzo Sauce 72
Shakshuka 50
Shrimp Paella 68
Spaghetti al Limone 56
Spiced Baked Rice with Fennel 57
Spiced Vegetable Couscous 58
Spice-Rubbed Pork Tenderloin with Fennel, Tomatoes, Olives, and Artichokes 73
Spicy Feta and Roasted Red Pepper Dip 99
Stewed Chickpeas with Eggplant and Tomatoes 78
Stuffed Calamari in Tomato Sauce 64

T
Turkish Stuffed Apricots with Pistachios and Rose Water 107

V
Vegetarian Paella with Green Beans and Chickpeas 62

W
White Bean Dip with Garlic and Rosemary 98

Z
Zucchini Fritters with Yogurt 90